IELTS BOOSTER

ACADEMIC

Photocopiable exam resources for teachers

Deborah Hobbs and Susan Hutchison

WITH AUDIO

Cambridge University Press and Assessment
www.cambridge.org/elt

Cambridge Assessment English
www.cambridgeenglish.org

Information on this title: www.cambridge.org/9781009249065

First published 2022

20   19   18   17   16   15   14   13   12   11   10   9   8   7   6   5   4   3   2   1

Printed in India by Multivista Global Pvt Ltd.

A catalogue record for this publication is available from the British Library

The publishers have no responsibility for the persistence or accuracy of URLs
for external or third-party internet websites referred to in this publication, and
do not guarantee that any content on such websites is, or will remain, accurate
or appropriate. Information regarding prices, travel timetables, and other factual
information given in this work is correct at the time of first printing but the
publishers do not guarantee the accuracy of such information thereafter.

CONTENTS

MAP OF THE BOOK

Writing

	Topic and task type
Worksheet 1 **Pages 53–56**	**Describing trends** Pie charts Describing numbers Making comparisons
Worksheet 2 **Pages 57–61**	**Describing a process** Writing a summary Present simple passive Grammatical range and accuracy Presenting an overview
Worksheet 3 **Pages 62–67**	**Discussion essay** Presenting an argument Supporting a point Following a plan Writing an introduction and a conclusion
Worksheet 4 **Pages 68–73**	**Advantages and disadvantages** Paraphrases Opposite views Writing a conclusion
Worksheet 5 **Pages 74–80**	**Double question essay** Agreeing or disagreeing Linking words

Speaking

	Topic and task type
Worksheet 1 **Pages 81–84**	**Friends and family** Speaking Part 1 Words and phrases to give examples Words and phrases to give reasons Appropriate answers
Worksheet 2 **Pages 85–88**	**Descriptions** Speaking Part 2 Linking language Making notes Coherence and fluency
Worksheet 3 **Pages 89–92**	**Discussion topics** Developing ideas Phrases to agree and disagree Developing your ideas

Think about it p93

Extended answer key p102

For useful information about preparing for the IELTS test, go to: weloveielts.org

HOW TO USE THE IELTS BOOSTER

Welcome to the IELTS Booster Academic

What is the IELTS Booster?

The IELTS Booster provides focused test practice on all parts of the IELTS test. It will help you to prepare for the test and gain the confidence, skills and knowledge you need for test day.

How can I use it?

Pick and choose the areas you want to practise at any time.

Use the IELTS Booster alongside a coursebook or on its own as a self-study tool.

Photocopy worksheets for ease of use.

How is it structured?

There are four sections which follow the order of the exam: Listening, Reading, Writing and Speaking.

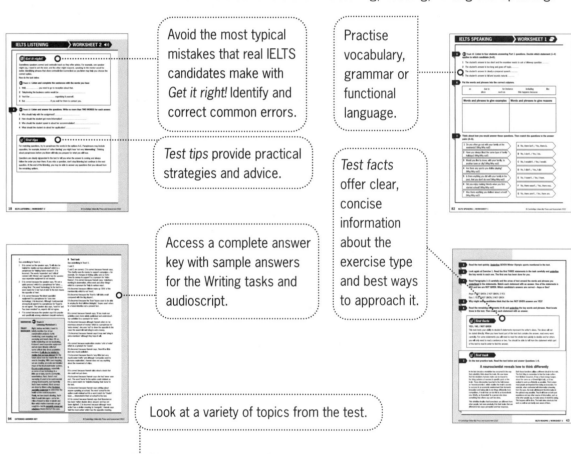

Avoid the most typical mistakes that real IELTS candidates make with *Get it right!* Identify and correct common errors.

Practise vocabulary, grammar or functional language.

Test tips provide practical strategies and advice.

Access a complete answer key with sample answers for the Writing tasks and audioscript.

Test facts offer clear, concise information about the exercise type and best ways to approach it.

Look at a variety of topics from the test.

For the audio, scratch the panel to see the code on the inside front cover. Go to cambridgeone.org or scan the QR code.

Find parts and exercises easily. There are several worksheets for each test part.

Think about it exercises help you understand how to approach each question type.

THE IELTS TEST

What are the two types of IELTS test?

The two types of tests are IELTS Academic and IELTS General Training. Both test English language abilities in Listening, Reading, Writing and Speaking. The Listening and Speaking parts are the same for both tests, but the Reading and Writing parts are different.

IELTS Academic is suitable:

- for studying at an English-speaking university, or other higher educational institution, at under- or postgraduate level.
- for professional registration, e.g., to register as an engineer, nurse or accountant in an English-speaking country.

IELTS General Training is suitable:

- for migration to certain English-speaking countries, like Canada or New Zealand.
- for studying below degree level in an English-speaking country.
- for a work placement in an English-speaking country or your own country.

How can I take the IELTS test?

You can take the IELTS test on paper or on a computer.

For IELTS on Paper, the Listening, Reading and Writing are completed on the same day and there are no breaks between them. The Speaking test can be completed up to seven days before or after. The total test time is 2 hours and 45 minutes.

For IELTS on Computer, the content and structure is the same as the paper test. You take the Listening, Reading and Writing test on the computer and the Speaking test is with an examiner face-to-face. The timings are a little different from the paper test as you do not have to transfer your answers to an answer sheet.

For more information about which test is suitable for you, and to check which organisations accept IELTS go to ielts.org.

TEST OVERVIEW

Listening 🔊

approximately 30 minutes

Speakers will have a range of native English accents, including British, North American and Australian. You'll hear the listening **once only.**

The Listening has a total of 40 questions and is in four parts. Each part has 10 questions.

Part 1 – a conversation between two people about an everyday topic (e.g., finding out information about a job)

Part 2 – a monologue about an everyday topic (e.g., giving information about changes in a community)

Part 3 – a conversation, usually between two people, in a training or educational context (e.g., students discussing an assignment)

Part 4 – a monologue in an academic context (e.g., a lecture)

Below are the question types you might find in the Listening:

Question type	Task format	Task focus
1 **Multiple choice**	Choose one answer from three alternatives, A–C. Choose two answers from five alternatives, A–E.	Tests detailed understanding of specific points or the overall understanding of the main points.
2 **Matching**	Match a list of statements with a set of options in a box.	Tests the ability to listen for detail and information provided.
3 **Plan, map, diagram labelling**	Label a plan, map or diagram, with a list provided in the question paper.	Tests the ability to understand a description of a place which is represented visually, e.g., the ability to understand and follow directions.
4 **Form, note, table, flowchart, summary completion**	Complete a form, notes, a table, a flowchart or a summary with a word or words from the Listening text.*	Tests the ability to understand and record the main points of the text in different formats.
5 **Sentence completion**	Complete a set of sentences using a word or words from the Listening text.*	Tests the ability to understand the main points in a text, e.g., cause and effect.
6 **Short-answer questions**	Read a question and then answer it with a short answer from the Listening text.*	Tests the ability to understand facts, e.g., places, dates and times.

*Candidates will hear the word they need in the text, and do not need to change it. They will be penalised if they go over the word limit given in the question, e.g., 'Write ONE WORD ONLY for each answer.'

Academic Reading 📖

60 minutes

IELTS Academic reading has a total of 40 questions. There are three long texts which range from descriptive to factual and discursive to analytical. Below are the question types you might find:

Question type	Task format	Task focus
1 Multiple choice	Choose one answer from four alternatives, A–D. Choose two answers from five alternatives, A–E. Choose three answers from seven alternatives, A–G.	Tests detailed understanding of specific points or the overall understanding of the main points.
2 Identifying information	Write whether a statement is confirmed (True), states the opposite (False) or is neither confirmed nor contradicted (Not Given).	Tests the ability to identify specific information in a text.
3 Identifying writers' views/claims	Write whether a statement agrees with the claim or view (Yes), disagrees with the claim or view (No), or the claim or view is neither confirmed nor contradicted (Not Given).	Tests the ability to identify ideas and opinions.
4 Matching information	Match information to a paragraph or section of the text.	Tests the ability to scan for specific information in a text.
5 Matching headings	Match headings to the correct paragraph or section. There are always more headings than you need.	Tests the ability to recognise the main topic or idea of a paragraph or section.
6 Matching features	Match a list of statements to a list of possible answers in a box (e.g., match research findings to researchers). Some options might not be used.	Tests the ability to scan and to understand facts and opinions in a text.
7 Matching sentence endings	Choose the best way to complete a sentence from a list of options. There are more options than questions.	Tests the ability to understand the main ideas in a text.
8 Sentence completion	Complete a sentence with a word or words from the text.	Tests the ability to find specific information.
9 Summary, note, table, flowchart completion	Complete a summary, notes, a table or a flowchart with a word or words from the text.	Tests the ability to understand details and main ideas of a text.
10 Diagram label completion	Label a diagram with the correct word from the text or list of options.	Tests the ability to understand a description and to transfer information to a diagram.
11 Short answer questions	Read a question and then answer with a short answer from the text.	Tests the ability to understand facts, e.g., places, dates and times.

Correct answers are worth one mark each.

© Cambridge University Press and Assessment 2022

TEST OVERVIEW

Academic Writing   60 minutes

There are two writing tasks, and you must answer both. Aim to take about 20 minutes to answer Task 1 and 40 minutes to answer Task 2.

Task	Number of words	Task format
Writing Task 1	at least 150	You need to accurately describe and summarise visual information which might be presented in one or more charts, tables, graphs or diagrams. This might include describing facts and figures or a process.
Writing Task 2	at least 250	You need to write a discursive essay in response to an opinion, problem or issue. This might include providing a solution, evaluating a problem, challenging a point of view or contrasting two opposing ideas.

You will be assessed on the following criteria:

Writing Task 1	Task achievement	Coherence and cohesion	Lexical resource	Grammatical range and accuracy
Writing Task 2	Task response	Coherence and cohesion	Lexical resource	Grammatical range and accuracy

Each task is assessed independently. The assessment of Task 2 carries more weight in marking than Task 1.

Speaking   11–14 minutes

The test consists of a face-to-face interview with an examiner. Tests are in three parts and are recorded.

Task	Timing	Task format
Speaking Part 1 – Interview	4–5 minutes	You answer questions on familiar topics, e.g., family, hobbies, likes and dislikes.
Speaking Part 2 – Long turn	3–4 minutes (including 1 minute preparation time)	You are given a task card, e.g., 'Describe something you want to own'. You have one minute to make notes before talking for up to two minutes.
Speaking Part 3 – Discussion	4–5 minutes	The examiner will ask you more abstract questions about the topic in Task 2, e.g., 'Does owning lots of possessions make people happy?'

You will be assessed on the following criteria:

Fluency and coherence	**Lexical resource**	**Grammatical range and accuracy**	**Pronunciation**
How well you maintain your flow of speech; how logical your answer is; how well you connect your ideas	The accuracy and variety of the vocabulary you use	The range, accuracy and complexity of the grammar you use	How intelligible you are

HOW IS IELTS SCORED?

You'll be awarded a band score of between 0 and 9 for your overall language ability. In addition, you'll be awarded an individual band score of between 0 and 9 for each of the four skills: Listening, Reading, Writing and Speaking. All scores are recorded on the Test Report Form along with details of your nationality, first language and date of birth. Each of the nine bands corresponds to a descriptive summary of your English language ability:

9 **Expert User** – *has fully operational command of the language. Their use of English is appropriate, accurate and fluent, and shows complete understanding.*

8 **Very Good User** – *has fully operational command of the language with only occasional unsystematic inaccuracies and inappropriate usage. They may misunderstand some things in unfamiliar situations. They handle complex and detailed argumentation well.*

7 **Good User** – *has operational command of the language, though with occasional inaccuracies, inappropriate usage and misunderstandings in some situations. They generally handle complex language well and understand detailed reasoning.*

6 **Competent User** – *has an effective command of the language despite some inaccuracies, inappropriate usage and misunderstandings. They can use and understand fairly complex language, particularly in familiar situations.*

5 **Modest User** – *has a partial command of the language and copes with overall meaning in most situations, although they are likely to make many mistakes. They should be able to handle basic communication in their own field.*

4 **Limited User** – *basic competence is limited to familiar situations. They have frequent problems in understanding and expression. They are not able to use complex language.*

3 **Extremely Limited User** – *conveys and understands only general meaning in very familiar situations. Frequent breakdowns in communication occur.*

2 **Intermittent User** – *has great difficulty understanding spoken and written English.*

1 **Non User** – *essentially has no ability to use the language beyond possibly a few isolated words.*

0 **Did not attempt the test** – *did not answer the questions.*

Most English-speaking universities accept an overall band score of between 6 and 7 for enrolment on degree courses. You should check which overall and individual band scores you need directly with the university or organisation you intend to apply to.

Dolphins

1 🔊 **Track 1 Do the short quiz about dolphins. Then listen and check your answers.**

---

1 Dolphins use their teeth to

    A catch their food ☐   **B** chew their food ☐

2 Why do they sleep with half their brain awake?

    A so they can breathe ☐   **B** so they can digest what they have eaten ☐

3 What is interesting about their skin?

    A it is hard ☐   **B** it is delicate ☐

---

2 🔊 **Track 1 Listen again and (circle) the correct option.**

1 Humans / Dolphins chew their food.

2 Swimming / Digestion does not happen while dolphins sleep.

3 Hard / Soft surfaces can damage dolphins' skin.

3 🔊 **Track 2 Listen to the next part of the talk and answer the question. Listen carefully as you will hear all the options but only one will be correct.**

On which day will the volunteers help with a research project?

A Wednesday ☐

B Thursday ☐

C Friday ☐

4 **Look at the four phrases from the talk you heard in Exercise 3. Select the phrases which may have made you choose an incorrect option because of word matching.**

1 project doesn't start ☐

2 researchers are examining ☐

3 dolphin's heart rate ☐

4 help feed and care for ☐

5 🔊 **Track 3 Listen to four short extracts. As you listen, write down the four paraphrases you hear.**

1 aim to keep safe ....

2 raise awareness of the problems ....

3 meet sea turtles, feed penguins and care for sick seals. ....

4 takes up most of our finances ....

6a You are going to listen to the rest of the talk. Before you do, look at the extract below and <u>underline</u> any words that might make you select Option A because of word matching. Option A is one of the options you will be looking at in the next exercise.

Extract: 'It used to be controversial among local experts, but thankfully that's been resolved.'
Option A: Experts do not agree about its value.

6b Look at the extract in Exercise 6a again. Read it carefully and think about meaning. Why is Option A an incorrect option? Discuss with a partner.

7  Track 4 Now listen to the rest of the talk.

What comment is made about each of the following projects?

Choose four comments from the box and write the correct letters (A–F) next to Questions 1–4. Two options are not needed. The questions follow the order you hear them.

Comments	
A Experts do not agree about its value.	**D** It takes quite a long time.
B It is helping future research.	**E** Money is urgently needed.
C It uses new technology.	**F** A lot of volunteers want to do it.

Projects

1 turtle monitoring ....
2 cave mapping ....
3 reef surveying ....
4 beach clear ....

> ☑ **Test tips**
>
> When answering multiple-choice questions, don't choose an answer because it includes the same word you hear (word matching). Instead look for the option which expresses the same idea as the speaker but in a different way. Note that the questions will appear in the order you hear them.

☑ **Test task**

8 🔊 Track 5 **Do the test practice task. Listen to a radio interview and answer the questions. Remember to listen for paraphrases and avoid word matching.**

Questions 1 and 2
Choose TWO letters, A–E
Which TWO things does Hannah say about the Dolphin Conservation Trust?

A Children make up most of the membership.

B It is the country's largest conservation organisation.

C It helps finance campaigns for changes in fishing practices.

D It employs several dolphin experts full time.

E Volunteers help in various ways.

....

Questions 3–5
Choose the correct letter, A, B, or C.

3 Why is Hannah so pleased the Trust has won the Charity Commission award?

    A It has brought in extra money.

    B It made the work of the Trust better known.

    C It has attracted more members.

4 Hannah says that a project in Scotland is causing problems for dolphins because of

    A sound.

    B oil leaks.

    C movement of ships.

5 Hannah became interested in dolphins when

    A she saw one swimming near her home.

    B she read a book about them.

    C she heard a speaker at her school.

Questions 6–9

What comment does Hannah make about each of the following dolphins?

Choose **FOUR** answers from the box and write the correct letter, A–F, next to Questions 6–9.

Two options are not needed. The questions follow the order you hear them.

Comments

A It has a loving personality.

B It is photographed frequently.

C It is always very energetic.

D It has not been seen this year.

E It is the newest to the scheme.

F It has an unusual shape.

Dolphins

6 Moondancer ....

7 Echo ....

8 Kiwi ....

9 Samson ....

Studying and work

A    **B**    **C**

1 Match the photos (A–C) to one of the situations (1–3).

1 studying abroad   ....

2 distance learning   ....

3 work placement   ....

2 ◀)) Track 6 **Listen. Which situation from Exercise 1 does the speaker want to discuss?**

....

3 ◀)) Track 7 **Look at the words and think about a suitable paraphrase. Then listen and write down the paraphrases you hear. You can listen more than once.**

Advice	
1 find something that is enjoyable	....
2 think about your future goals	....
3 show ability in the subject	....
4 make sure you work hard	....
5 get help	....

4 Look at the questions (1–5) and <u>underline</u> the words you think will be signposted in the listening text. The first one has been done for you.

Stages in doing a year abroad

1 in the <u>second year</u> of the course

2 when first choosing where to go

3 when sending your choices

4 when writing your personal statement

5 when doing the year abroad

5 ◀)) Track 8 **Listen to the short excerpt from a conversation between two students, Mia and Josh. Which question from Exercise 4 is Mia talking about?**

6 🔊 Track 9 **Now listen to the first part of the same conversation and choose the correct option. Remember to listen carefully as soon as you hear the words that tell you (signpost) when the answer is coming.**

1 In the second year of the course Josh should

    A make travel arrangements and bookings.

    B show ability in Theatre Studies.

7a **You are going to listen to the whole conversation between Mia and Josh. Before you listen, look at the remaining options and write down the paraphrases you might hear. B has been done for you.**

Actions	
A make travel arrangements and bookings	....
B show ability in Theatre Studies	*get good marks and know the subject well* ....
C be on time	....
D get a letter of recommendation	....
E plan for the final year	....
F make sure the focus of the course is relevant	....
G ask for help	....

7b 🔊 Track 10 **Now listen. Choose FOUR answers from the box in Exercise 7a and write the correct letter next to Questions 2–5. Remember there will always be options that you do not need. Question 1 has been done for you.**

Stages in doing a 'year abroad'

1 in the second year of the course   .B......

2 when choosing where to go   ....

3 when sending your choices   ....

4 when writing your personal statement   ....

5 when doing the year abroad   ....

⊙ Get it right!

Sometimes speakers correct and contradict each as they offer advice. For example, one speaker might say, *I need to ask the tutor*, and the other might respond, *speaking to the mentor would be better*. Identifying phrases that show contradiction (correction) as you listen may help you choose the correct option.

Now do the task below.

🔊 **Track 11** **Listen and complete the sentences with the words you hear.**

1 Well, ... you need to go to reception about that.

2 Telephoning the business centre would be ....

3 You'd be .... organising it yourself.

4 But .... if you wait for them to contact you.

8 🔊 **Track 12** **Listen and answer the questions. Write no more than TWO WORDS for each answer. Compare your answers with a partner.**

1 Who should help with the assignment? ....

2 How should the student get more information? ....

3 Who should the student speak to about her accommodation? ....

4 What should the student do about her application? ....

☑ Test tips

For matching questions, try to paraphrase the words in the options A–E. Paraphrases may include opposites, for example, instead of 'rather **boring**' you might hear 'not very **interesting**'. Thinking about paraphrases before you listen will help you prepare for what you will hear.

Questions are clearly signposted in the text to tell you when the answer is coming and always follow the order you hear them. If you miss a question, don't stop listening but continue to the next question. At the end of the listening, you may be able to answer any questions that you missed from the remaining options.

Test task

9 ◀)) Track 13 **Do the test practice task. Listen to the conversation about work placement and answer the questions. What source of information should Alex use at each of the following stages of the work placement?**

Choose SIX answers from the box and write the correct letter, A–G, next to Questions 1–6.

Stages of the work placement

A get updates

B discuss options

C supply a reference

D informing about outcome of interview

E responding to invitation for interview

F obtain company information

G register with STEP

Sources of information

1 careers officer ....

2 work experience fair ....

3 the internet ....

4 mentor ....

5 human resources department ....

6 personal tutor ....

Films and filmmaking

1 🔊 Track 14 **What do you know about films and filmmaking? Complete the short quiz with a partner, then listen and check your answers. You can listen more than once.**

---

1 A 'mainstream' film can be described as

A a film with lots of special effects. ☐

B a film made by a large production company. ☐

2 What type of films enter film festival competitions?

A independent films ☐

B studio films ☐

3 Most studio films are funded by

A private investors and individuals. ☐

B the studio that is making them. ☐

4 Film production consists of

A seven stages. ☐

B ten stages. ☐

---

2 **Look at the flowchart opposite and answer the questions with no more than TWO WORDS. Do not fill in the gaps in the flowchart just yet.**

1 What process is being described? ....

2 How many steps are there in the process? ....

3 Do you need to answer a question in each stage? ....

4 For the third gap, do you need a singular or plural noun? ....

Video animation process

Hold a meeting with the **1** ....

↓

Create a video **2** .... and write the script.

↓

Go online and find an actor with a suitable **3** ....

↓

Produce a storyboard using **4** .... of the stages of the story.

↓

Develop the visual style by including **5** .... and background images.

↓

Do the animation to add life to the images.

↓

To create mood, add **6** ....

---

3 🔊 Track 15 **Listen to the first part of a conversation between two students, Ria and Stan. As you listen, fill in the first gap (1) in the flowchart in Exercise 2. Write ONE WORD ONLY.**

4 🔊 Track 15 **Listen again. What words do you hear that tell you the answer is coming?**

A Have you got a minute? ☐

B I'm not too sure about all the stages. ☐

C The first thing is … ☐

5 🔊 Track 16 **Now listen to the whole conversation between Ria and Stan, and fill in the remaining gaps (2–6) in the flowchart in Exercise 2. Write ONE WORD ONLY for each answer.**

6 🔊 Track 16 **Ria and Stan use signposting language which will help you follow what they are saying. Complete the sentences from the conversation with the words in the box. Then listen to the conversation from Exercise 5 again and check your answers.**

finish	following	move	once	that	then

1 Next, we .... on to the idea or concept stage.

2 Then, ... that's been agreed, we start writing the script.

3 We .... have to find an actor.

4 After .... , a storyboard is put together.

5 The .... step, animation, is probably my favourite.

6 Before we .... , we can set the mood by adding the right music.

7 **Track 17 Listen to the extracts and complete the sentences with ONE WORD ONLY.**

1 To .... this point, let me tell you about what I did at the film studio.

2 This brings me to my .... point, which is the development of special effects.

3 So, in other .... , the reason I chose film studies was because …

4 OK, so we've .... at the challenges of scriptwriting …

5 I'd like to .... by describing the film production process.

6 I've .... about the role of the director …

☑ *Test tips*

When giving a presentation or lecture, speakers often use signposting language to connect their ideas and move between topics. Listening for signposting language as well as using the headings and subheadings on the question paper will help you follow the speaker and answer the questions correctly.

---

8 **Match the extracts (1–6) in Exercise 7 to their uses (A–D) below.**

A to start a new topic   ....

B to give an example   ....

C to paraphrase and clarify   ....

D to finish a topic   ....

Test task

9 🔊 **Track 18 Listen to a presentation about film production and complete the flowchart below. Write ONE WORD ONLY for each answer. Remember, listen for signposting and use the subheadings to help you follow the speaker.**

The stages of film production

Development

Projects begin with development of a **1** .... based on a book or other source. Writers produce an outline.

⬇

Pre-production

Production options are reduced and **2** .... starts.

3 .... are employed.

⬇

Production

A schedule must be followed so there are no problems with the **4** ....

5 .... is very important.

⬇

Photography

An expensive stage because of things like **6** .... and filming in

7 .... places.

⬇

Wrap

The set is taken down, the site cleared, and goods are returned to **8** ....

⬇

Postproduction

Film footage is in the **9** ....

⬇

Distribution

Producers recover their investments. Films are sent to **10** .... or online platforms.

Maps

1 Look at the photos (A–C) and match them to the most appropriate sentences (1–3).

A

B

C

1 Take the left fork. ....

2 Follow the road, round the bend. ....

3 Turn right at the junction. ....

2a 🔊 Track 19 Look at the three maps (A, B and C). Listen and decide which map shows the directions that the speaker gives.

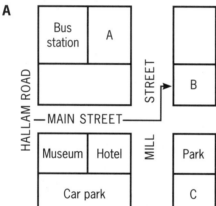

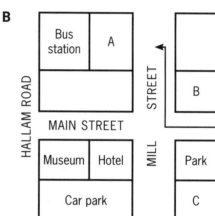

2b 🔊 Track 19 Listen again and complete the phrases. Use no more than THREE WORDS.

1 Right. Well, ... Main Street.

2 .... at the lights.

3 It's .... the park.

(●) Get it right!

For map labelling questions, you will need to understand and follow directions. Familiarising yourself with the language of location and direction will help you follow the speaker.

🔊 **Track 20 Complete the phrases with the words in the box. Then listen and check your answers.**

alongside	before	centre	over	rear	round	through	up

1 Walk .... this road until you reach the lights.

2 Go .... the door on the right.

3 Just .... the bend you will find the coffee shop.

4 Go .... the bridge and into the forest.

5 Enter via the .... of the building.

6 You'll find the fountain in the .... of the park.

7 Just .... you reach the lake, there is the picnic area.

8 The river runs .... the railway line.

3 🔊 **Track 21 Look at the map and the candidate's answers. The candidate has answered two questions incorrectly and one correctly. Listen and put a tick (✓) next to the correct answer and write the correct letter (A–G) next to the incorrect answers. Compare your answers with a partner.**

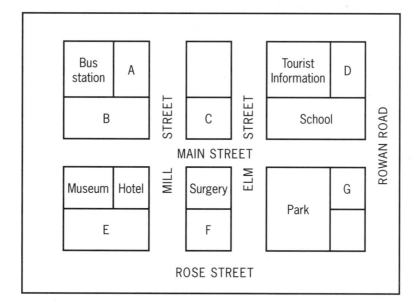

1 bank ....D.......... **2** coffee shop ....C.......... **3** science centre ...A..........

4 ▶ 🔊 **Track 22** Listen to extracts from a talk about planned improvements to a town called Red Hill. Correct the <u>underlined</u> words with what the speaker actually says.

1 The trees will be located <u>opposite</u> the supermarket. ....

2 Pavements <u>at the junction of</u> Carberry Street ... .

3 Traffic lights will be installed <u>at the end of</u> Hill Street. ....

5 ▶ 🔊 **Track 23** **The map below shows the planned improvements to Red Hill. Listen and write the correct letters (A–H) next to Questions 1–7. The questions follow the order of the talk. There is one letter you do not need.**

Red Hill Improvement Plan

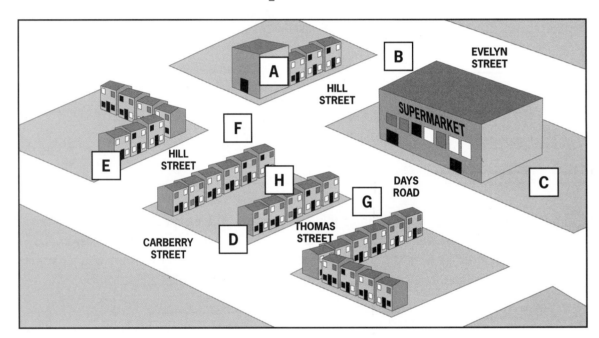

1 trees ....

2 wider pavements ....

3 painted road surface ....

4 new sign ....

5 traffic lights ....

6 paintings ....

7 children's playground ....

Test tips

If you are given a compass icon showing north, south, east and west, it is likely you will hear phrases like 'in the west' and 'to the south'. Use them to help orientate and direct you.

6 ▶ **Look at the map below. Complete the sentences with the correct phrases.**

in the far northwest   in the southeast   just on the west   near the north   south of   to the east

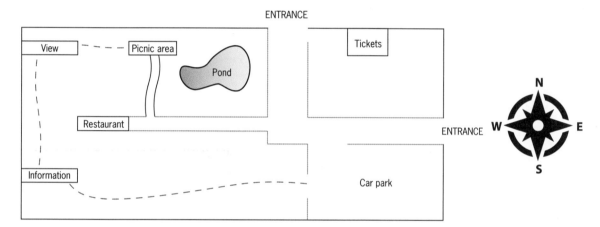

1 The car park is .... corner.

2 There's a viewpoint .... of the park.

3 .... of the viewpoint, you'll find the picnic area.

4 A little .... the picnic area, past the fishpond, is the restaurant.

5 There's a small path, ... edge of car park which goes to the information centre.

6 .... entrance is the ticket office.

☑ **Test task**

7 🔊 Track 24 **Label the map below. Listen and write the correct letters (A–I) next to Questions 1–5.**

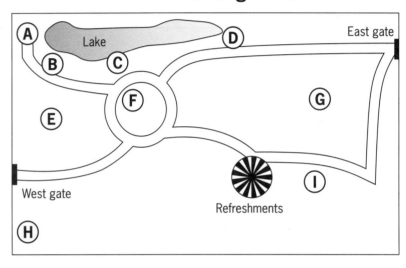

Hinchingbrooke Park

1 bird hide ....

2 dog walking ....

3 flower garden ....

4 wood ....

5 toilets ....

Animals in the wild

1 🔊 Track 25 **Look at the photos.**

What do you think the animals have in common? Discuss with a partner.

Listen to the beginning of a conversation between Kennie and Anna, and check your ideas.

◎ Get it right!

In IELTS Listening, candidates often lose marks because they have made simple mistakes, for example, they have ignored the word limit or they have not checked whether a singular or plural noun form is needed. Make sure you read instructions carefully, use headings (if there are any) and check your answers before you transfer them to the answer sheet.

a Look at the table and instructions. Four of the answers (1–6) are incorrect because the candidate has made simple mistakes and two are correct. Put a cross (✗) next to the candidate's 'incorrect' answers and a tick (✓) next to the correct ones.

Write NO MORE THAN TWO WORDS for each answer.

<table>
<tr><th colspan="4">Tilly's Tours</th></tr>
<tr><th>Day</th><th>Event</th><th>Venue</th><th>Information</th></tr>
<tr><td>Monday</td><td>**1** The river walk</td><td>Central Park</td><td>There is a **2** small £10 charge</td></tr>
<tr><td>Tuesday</td><td>**3** Wednesday</td><td>Gallery</td><td>There are no **4** camera allowed</td></tr>
<tr><td>**5** Saturday</td><td>Whale watching</td><td>Aquarium</td><td>Children cannot feed **6** the animals</td></tr>
</table>

b Now match the common candidate errors in the table with the reasons for the errors (A–C) below.

A The candidate did not follow the instructions. ....

B The candidate did not write the exact word they heard. ....

C The candidate did not use the headings to help them. ....

2 ➤ **Delete the incorrect option.**

1 Leylah wants to buy these book / books for her IELTS class.

2 I have some concern / concerns about the test.

3 Either boy / boys can help you paint the door.

4 I'm not sure if both girl / girls went to school yesterday.

5 When she went on holiday to Rome, she visited a number of museum / museums.

6 That's the third time this week! Why do you arrive late every day / days?

7 He's in the park with one of his dog / dogs now.

8 It's time we started to protect these animal / animals.

9 I have several idea / ideas to share with you.

10 That was the main thing / things I wanted to tell you.

3 ➤ **Look at the table in Exercise 4 and read the instructions and headings carefully. Ask yourself one or two questions using the information on either side of the gaps and write them down. Use the question words 'What', 'Why', 'Where', 'Who', etc. Examples for the first two have been done for you.**

1 *What part of a shark (noun) might a pattern cover? What part of a shark might help it move easily?*

2 *Where might part of a shark be used by humans?*

3 ....

4 ....

5 ....

6 ....

4 ➤ 🔊 **Track 26 Now listen to the whole conversation between Kennie and Anna that you heard the beginning of in Exercise 1. As you listen, complete the table. Remember to use the headings and information provided to help you follow the speakers and hear the correct answers. Write ONE WORD ONLY for each answer.**

Animal	Reasons for scientific interest	Human use
Shark	A pattern covering its **1** .... helps it move easily.	Used on the bottom of **2** ....
Gecko	**3** .... on their feet allow them to stick to smooth surfaces.	**4** .... have been made for climbers. Plans for use in space.
Kingfisher	Aerodynamic: They can **5** .... silently because of the shape of their beak.	Japanese high-speed trains are quiet in **6** ....

Test tips

When answering table completion questions, use the time before you listen to look at the instructions and headings, and think about the type of words (or numbers) you are listening for. Asking yourself questions, using the information on either side of the gap (if there is any), might increase your understanding and help you hear the correct answer when you listen.

Test task

5 ◀)) Track 27 **Questions 1–7. Listen and complete the table below.**

Write ONE WORD ONLY for each answer.

Animals	Reasons for population increase in gardens	Comments
1	Appropriate stretches of water	Massive increase in urban population
Hedgehogs	Safer from **2** .... in cities	Easy to **3** .... them accurately
Song thrushes	A variety of **4** .... to eat More nesting places available	A large **5** .... starting soon
Peregrine falcon	Less use of **6**	Possible to watch them **7** ....

Design competition

1 🔊 Track 28 **Read the dos and don'ts, and predict a suitable word for each gap. Then listen and check your answers.**

Note completion

Do

1 Use any headings to .... you follow the speaker.

2 Think about the type of .... you need, for example a place.

3 Listen for specific ....

4 Remember the answers will come in the .... you hear them.

Don't

5 Waste .... as you are listening.

6 Leave any question .... : guess if you are not sure.

7 .... anything the speaker says, for example write 'frog' if you hear 'frogs'.

---

2 🔊 Track 28 **Listen again and write the paraphrases or synonyms you hear for these phrases.**

1 use the headings

....

2 think about

....

3 remember that the answers

....

4 as you are listening

....

5 if you are not sure

....

3 **Which phrase told you the speaker was moving to the final point. Choose the correct option.**

A right, next I'd say ☐

B one more thing ☐

C that's a big mistake ☐

4 Look at the <u>underlined</u> words and write down synonyms or paraphrases you might hear. The first one has been done for you. Don't worry about the answering the questions (1–5) yet.

Global Design Competition

Jonas's **1** .... told Jonas to <u>get help</u>. find support ....

The professor has received Jonas's **2** .... <u>by email</u>. ....

Jonas is <u>designing a device</u> that can be used at home in a **3** ....

Jonas aims to use **4** .... <u>in a new way</u>. ....

Jonas believes **5** .... are <u>similar</u> and <u>not very interesting</u>.

....

---

5 Look at the sentences in Exercise 4 again. Predict what type of word is needed in each gap and write it down. The first one has been done for you.

Sentence 1   a person ....

Sentence 2   ....

Sentence 3   ....

Sentence 4   ....

Sentence 5   ....

6a Look at an excerpt from the listening. <u>Underline</u> the word in the excerpt that fits in the first gap in Exercise 4.

JONAS: Hello professor. I'm working on my entry for the Global Design Competition.

My tutor said you might be able to give me some support.

6b 🔊 Track 29 Now listen and complete the sentences (2–5) in Exercise 4 with ONE WORD only. Write down the exact word you hear and remember the questions follow the order of the conversation.

Test tips

Before you listen, look at the questions and consider what paraphrases or synonyms you might hear. Identifying paraphrases as you listen will help you 'hear' when the correct answer is coming.

Test task

7 🔊 Track 30 **Listen to the final part of Jonas's conversation with his professor and complete the notes below.**

Write ONE WORD ONLY for each answer.

Global Design Competition

'The Rockpool'

- The stone in Jonas's design is used for **1** .... the machine.
- Carbon dioxide is used to **2** .... the dishes.
- At the end of the washing cycle, **3** .... goes into a holding chamber.
- Jonas thinks his idea has a lot of **4** .... to reduce household costs.

Entry submission

- Jonas needs help preparing for his **5** ....
- The professor advises Jonas to make a **6** .... of his design.
- Jonas's main problem is getting good quality **7** ....
- The professor suggests Jonas apply for a **8** ....
- The professor will check the **9** .... in Jonas's written report.

Read quickly through the following text and scan the questions.

A unique species of seahorse

A   On the island of Eleuthera in The Bahamas, in the Caribbean Sea, there is a special pool of water. Its location is a bit of a hidden secret and local people are keen to keep it that way, at least for now. Known locally as Sweetings Pond, this stretch of water is 1.5km wide, 2.5km from end to end and a mere 13m in depth. Within its shadowy waters lives a collection of sea creatures including crabs and octopuses. But the most incredible of all, this little-surveyed ecosystem is home to the world's largest known population of seahorses.

'At first you may not think there's anything there,' says Shane Goss, an underwater photographer who knows the pool well. With their heads hunched down and colours matching their surroundings, seahorses are masters of disguise, looking a lot like clams or mussels. When Goss brings friends to snorkel in the pool, they can spend ages searching in vain for seahorses. But as soon he points one out and they know what to look for, they realise these creatures are everywhere. 'They'll spot one every minute or two after that,' he says. Nowhere in the world will you have a better chance of spotting these curious little fish.

B   Counting how many seahorses live in the pool is not an easy task. 'Mark and recapture' is a classic technique for estimating animal numbers and often works well for seahorses. The procedure involves carefully catching the creatures, injecting a dot of harmless coloured dye under their skin, then letting them go again. Repeat visits to the area will provide an estimate of how many animals come and go, and a rough idea of the total population size.

Using this same method, seahorse biologist Dr Heather Masonjones estimated that there were many thousands of seahorses inhabiting the pool. Because of their particularly active nature, she experienced some trouble finding the marked seahorses again. While she has yet to come up with

a definitive number of seahorses, she is confident that the pool is home to the most densely populated community of seahorses in the world. This is likely because the pool is in such a secluded setting. And this relative isolation has resulted in a lack of predators, meaning that young seahorses have a greater chance of reaching adulthood.

C   How seahorses originally arrived in the pool remains a mystery. It seems incredible that these sea creatures could not only survive, but thrive, in a land-locked pool. Sweetings Pond <u>is technically known as</u> an 'anchialine' pool. The water is salty as the pool is connected to the open sea by porous rock and <u>it may be that</u> a few young seahorses managed to swim through these holes in the rock separating the two bodies of water. Or <u>it could be the case that</u> somebody put them there. There <u>is a long history</u> of people in the Bahamas using natural pools for informal aquaculture, perhaps stocking them with fish to grow bigger and multiply. <u>One other theory is that</u> they were left behind by falling sea-levels in the past. All that we <u>know for sure is</u> that they are there now, and in very large numbers.

Another great puzzle surrounds the true identity of the seahorses. When Dr Masonjones first visited the pool, she wasn't sure which species they belonged to. There are two large Atlantic species in the Bahamas: *Hippocampus reidi*, which have long slim heads and bodies; and lined seahorses, *H. erectus*, which have shorter heads and stragglier spines. Both can grow to at least 17cm from head to tail, and neither is a close match to the ones living in the pool. Dr Masonjones first thought was that these seahorses looked like the two species put together. She began to wonder if the species were interbreeding, but genetic studies which involved sequencing two of the seahorses' genes showed that these are in fact lined seahorses, but unlike others of that species.

D   Living in their isolated pool, these seahorses seem to be heading down their own evolutionary path, in a similar way to animals on remote islands. These secluded creatures could be adjusting to the unusual environment of the pool, where conditions differ from the surrounding areas. For one thing, their tails are shorter and more stubbier than normal. This is likely because their self-contained environment lacks the currents of the open ocean and so it is much easier to swim in – this would also explain their active and highly mobile lifestyle. They also have longer, more slender heads than their open-seas cousins. This may have something to do with the way seahorses feed and the type of food available in the pool. They are not equipped with teeth so use a process known as 'pipette feeding' to eat tiny shrimps and plankton. With their swivelling eyes, they spot a target, slowly line up their head within striking range, then rapidly flick their snout upwards, sucking in the prey before it has a chance to escape into the golden beds of algae.

E Being so cut off puts the pool and its seahorses at particular risk. In recent years, there have been incidences of people deliberately removing them from the pool and the risk of that continuing is high because these creatures are unique and therefore very valuable. Another threat is the possibility that the pool could be turned into a marina – the Bahamas lacks protected harbours and there are plenty of people willing to pay good money for somewhere to moor up their boats. Seahorses are extremely vulnerable to these kinds of physical disturbances as they rely on one mating partner

over their lifetime and when they are separated from their life partner, it can seriously affect their ability to sustain the population. Agricultural practices in the area are also moving increasingly close to the pool's borders, bringing real fears that chemical run-off from pesticides and fertilisers could contaminate the water quality.

F Raising local awareness of these threats is a vital part of conservation efforts to protect this unique ecosystem. And thankfully a sense of community pride is growing and there are people beginning to emerge who may play an important role in the pool's future. There are plans to take government officials and decision makers to the pool to meet scientists so that they get first-hand experience of why effectively managing access to the pool and reducing the threats matters. If this proves successful, then these special creatures will stay safe and sound, even if they are receiving more attention than they would normally like.

Read the questions but don't worry about doing this exercise yet.

Questions 1–6
Choose the correct letter, A, B, C or D.

1 What do we learn about the seahorses in Eleuthera in the first section?
 A They live in <u>deep</u> <u>waters</u>.
 B They can initially be difficult to spot.
 C They inhabit an area that is easily accessible.
 D They have been extensively studied.

2 According to the passage, the method used to count seahorses
 A can cause injury to the animal.
 B is seldom used on other species.
 C produces precise information.
 D takes a long time to complete.

3 What *fact* is given about the seahorses in Sweetings Pond in Section C?
 A They were first introduced there by local people.
 B They are distinct from other seahorses of the same species.
 C They originally arrived there in groups.
 D They ended up there due to a change in sea levels.

4 In Section D, the writer is trying to
 A explain how well the seahorses have adapted to their habitat.
 B describe how seahorses have expanded their diet over time.
 C contrast the physical conditions of the pool with the open sea in detail.
 D compare the feeding behaviour of the seahorses with that of other species.

5 In Section E, we learn that the seahorses are already affected by
 A pollution.   **B** harbour development.
 C hunting.   **D** farming methods.

6 What would be a suitable title for the text?
 A An extraordinary creature with no more secrets left to discover
 B A secretive animal facing the challenges of a changing world
 C An unusual species on the very brink of extinction
 D A forgotten fish overlooked by both researchers and local people

1a What can you remember about seahorses? Do the quiz.

Seahorses quiz

1 Seahorses are classified as
   A mammals. ☐   **B** fish. ☐

2 Where do they live?
   A in saltwater ☐   **B** in freshwater ☐

3 Their bodies are covered in
   A scales. ☐   **B** plates. ☐

4 Do seahorses have teeth?
   A yes ☐   **B** no ☐

5 They eat
   A shrimps. ☐   **B** algae. ☐

6 Over their lifetime, seahorses have
   A one partner. ☐   **B** many partners. ☐

1b Read the text quickly and check your guesses. The answers are in the same order as the text.

2 Read the four topic areas. Match each one with the correct section (A–D) of the text.

a system of assessment	Section A
the arrival of the seahorses into the pool	Section B
a little-known location	Section C
how the seahorses are developing	Section D

3a Read Sections E and F of the text. Think of a topic area for each of these sections.

Section E ....   Section F ....

3b Discuss your ideas with a partner. Were your ideas similar or different? Then compare them with the suggestions in the answer key.

4a Look at the questions below the text. Read Questions 1 and 2 carefully and <u>underline</u> the key words in the options. The first question has been <u>underlined</u> for you.

4b Think of different ways to express the key words you have <u>underlined</u> in Questions 1 and 2. Write your ideas next to each option (A–D). There is an example to help you.

   A They inhabit <u>deep</u> waters – not shallow ....
   B They can initially be difficult to spot. ....
   C They inhabit an area that is easily accessible. ....
   D They have been extensively studied. ....

4c   Read Sections A and B carefully and locate the parts of the text that relate to each option in Questions 1 and 2. The text that refers to Option A in Question 1 has been <u>underlined</u> for you.

4d   Read the options and the section of text you have highlighted and choose your answers to Questions 1 and 2.

4e   Look at two students' answers for Questions 1 and 2. Which student has answered both questions correctly?

     Jonas: 1 B; 2 D   **Daria:** 1 A; 2 C

5a   Look at the word 'fact' in Question 3 and look at the <u>underlined</u> areas of text in Section C. Which refer to 'facts' or things that are true and which refer to 'speculation' or things that may or may not be true?

5b   Choose your answer for Question 3 and check your answer.

6   Complete Questions 4 and 5. Then check your answers.

7a   Think about the text as a whole. Do you think it is generally positive or negative in tone? Why? Write down some reasons. Think of a title for the text and write it down.

7b   Look at Question 6 and compare your title with the options. Is your title similar to any of them?

7c   Choose your answer to Question 6 and then check your answer.

☑) *Test tips*

- Read the whole text quickly to get an idea of what it is about – it is a good idea to write down a phrase that describes the 'topic area' of each paragraph/section.
- Read the options for each question carefully as each of these will be referred to in the text.
- <u>Underline</u> the key words in the options.
- Try to think of synonyms for the key words where you can.

8 Do the test practice task. Read the text below and answer Questions 1–5.

When evolution runs backwards

A Evolution isn't supposed to run backwards – yet an increasing number of examples show that it does and that it can sometimes represent the future of a species.

The description of any animal as an 'evolutionary throwback' is controversial. For the better part of a century, most biologists have been reluctant to use those words, mindful of a principle of evolution that says 'evolution cannot run backwards'. But as more and more examples come to light and modern genetics enters the scene, that principle is having to be rewritten. Not only are evolutionary throwbacks possible, they sometimes play an important role in the forward march of evolution.

The technical term for an evolutionary throwback is an 'avatism', from the Latin *atavus*, meaning forefather. The word has ugly connotations thanks largely to Cesare Lombroso, a 19th-century Italian medic who argued that criminals were born not made and could be identified by certain physical features that were throwbacks to a primitive sub-human state.

B While Lombroso was measuring criminals, a Belgian palaeontologist called Louis Dollo was studying fossil records and coming to the opposite conclusion. In 1890 he proposed that evolution was irreversible: 'that an organism is unable to return, even partially, to a previous stage already realised in the ranks of its ancestors'. Early 20th-century biologists came to a similar conclusion, though they qualified it in terms of probability, stating there is no reason why evolution cannot run backwards – it is just very unlikely. And so the idea of irreversibility in evolution stuck and came to be known as 'Dollo's law'.

If Dollo's law is right, atavisms should occur only very rarely, if at all. Yet almost since the idea took root, exceptions have been cropping up. In 1919, for example, a humpback whale with a pair of leg-like appendages over a metre long, complete with a full set of limb bones, was caught off Vancouver Island in Canada. Explorer Roy Chapman Andrews argued at the time that the whale must be a throwback to a land-living ancestor. 'I can see no other explanation', he wrote in 1921.

C Since then, so many other examples have been discovered that it no longer makes sense to say that evolution is as good as irreversible. And this poses a puzzle: how can characteristics that disappeared millions of years ago suddenly reappear? In 1994, Rudolf Raff and colleagues at Indiana University in the USA decided to use genetics to put a number on the probability of evolution going into reverse. They reasoned that while some evolutionary changes involve the loss of genes and are therefore irreversible, others may be the result of genes being switched off. If these silent genes are somehow switched back on, they argued, long-lost traits could reappear.

Raff's team went on to calculate the likelihood of it happening. Silent genes accumulate random mutations, they reasoned, eventually rendering them useless. So how long can a gene survive in a species if it is no longer used? The team calculated that there is a good chance of silent genes surviving for up to 6 million years in at least a few individuals in a population, and that some might survive for as long as 10 million years. In other words, throwbacks are possible, but only to the relatively recent evolutionary past.

As a possible example, the team pointed to the mole salamanders of Mexico and California. Like most amphibians these begin life in a juvenile 'tadpole' state, then metamorphose into the adult form – except for one species, the axolotl, which famously lives its entire life as a juvenile. The simplest explanation for this is that the axolotl lineage alone lost the ability to metamorphose, while others retained it. From a detailed analysis of the salamanders' family tree, however, it is clear that the other lineages evolved from an ancestor that itself had lost the ability to metamorphose. In other words, metamorphosis in mole salamanders is an atavism. The salamander example fits with Raff's 10-million-year time frame.

D More recently, however, examples have been reported that break the time limit, suggesting that silent genes may not be the whole story. Biologist Gunter Wagner of Yale University reported some work on the evolutionary history of a group of South American lizards called Bachia. Many of these snakes have minuscule limbs; some look more like snakes than lizards and a few have completely lost the toes on their hind limbs.

Other species, however, sport up to four toes on their hind legs. The simplest explanation is that the toed lineages never lost their toes, but Wagner begs to differ. According to his analysis of the Bachia family tree, the toed species re-evolved toes from toeless ancestors and, what is more, digit loss and gain has occurred on more than one occasion over tens of millions of years.

Questions 1–5
Choose the correct letter, A, B, C or D.

1 What do we learn about the theory developed by Louis Dollo in Section B?

A It was immediately referred to as Dollo's law.

B It supported the possibility of evolutionary throwbacks.

C It was modified by biologists in the early 20th century.

D It was based on many years of research.

2 The humpback whale caught off Vancouver Island is mentioned because of

A the exceptional size of its body.

B the way it exemplifies Dollo's law.

C the amount of controversy it caused.

D the reason given for its unusual features.

3 What is said about 'silent genes' in Section C?

A Their numbers vary according to species.

B Raff disagreed with the use of the term.

C They could lead to the re-emergence of certain characteristics.

D They can have an unlimited lifespan.

4 The writer mentions the mole salamander because

A it exemplifies what happens in the development of most amphibians.

B it suggests that Raff's theory is correct.

C it has lost and regained more than one ability.

D its ancestors have become the subject of extensive research.

5 In Section D, Wagner claims that

A members of the Bachia family have lost and regained certain features several times.

B evidence shows that the evolution of the Bachia lizard is due to the environment.

C his research into South American lizards supports Raff's assertions.

D his findings will apply to other species of South American lizards.

Read quickly through the following text and scan the questions.

How a thrill-seeking personality helps Olympic athletes

One of the main draws of the Winter Olympics is the opportunity to witness some of the most exciting and nail-biting athletic feats. The daring events include the bobsled and downhill skiing. Then there's the terrifying skeleton: imagine barrelling down a narrow chute of twisted ice-coated concrete at 125 miles per hour. Now imagine doing that head first, like a human battering ram.

Athletes train for years for these events, but most of these elite athletes possess something that helps them succeed during these high-stakes events: their personality. They have a personality that enables them to focus in highly chaotic environments – like the ones you would see during the Winter Olympics. It's called a high sensation-seeking personality, and it's a trait that, as a psychologist, I've long been fascinated with.

To some extent, we all crave complex and novel sensations. Whether it's our attraction to the new burger place down the street, the latest shiny gadget or the newest fashion trend, novelty tugs at us. But even though we all share an interest in new sensations, what sets high sensation-seeking personalities apart is that they crave these exotic and intense experiences to an extent that they are willing to risk their health.

What's interesting is that some high sensation-seeking individuals experience less stress and appear fearless and calm in the face of danger. For example, 2014 Olympic slalom gold medallist Mikaela Shiffrin tears down mountains at speeds of 80 miles per hour. However, although she is travelling at high speeds, her perception of time changes to what feels like slow motion.

There is neurological evidence to back up the sense of calm that athletes like Shiffrin feel in the midst of chaos and danger. You may have heard of cortisol – this is the 'fight or flight' hormone, and it can make us feel stressed and overwhelmed. However, when people with high sensation-seeking personalities have intense experiences, they don't produce that much cortisol. On top of that, they produce higher levels of 'pleasure' chemicals like dopamine. What's more, researchers have found that people with high sensation-seeking personalities have increased sensitivity to things that could be rewarding, like landing a perfect double cork 1080 in skateboarding, and decreased sensitivity to potential dangers, like the fear of wiping out after attempting a triple axel jump in figure skating.

High sensation-seeking isn't exclusive to Winter Olympians, of course – it can creep into every aspect of life. For instance, it can influence the way you interact with other people, the things you do for fun, the music you like, the way you drive and even the jokes you tell.

In the 1950s, Canadian psychologists began studying sensory deprivation. In his lab at McGill University, Robert Zuckerman was interested in how people reacted to the loss of sensation. He placed his research subjects in environments where they could hear or see very little. For the first hour or so, all the participants just sat in the dark. But after a while, things changed. While some of them continued to sit quietly for hours, others became bored and anxious. Zuckerman was eventually able to show that sensation-seeking is made up of four distinct components. Each component contributes to an individual's unique way of seeking (or avoiding) sensation.

The first two components of the sensation-seeking personality are thrill-seeking and experience-seeking. However, the trait also involves disinhibition and boredom susceptibility. Disinhibition has to do with our willingness to be spontaneous and our ability to let loose. People with low levels of disinhibition always look before they leap, they are cautious, unlike those with high disinhibition who will do the opposite. Boredom susceptibility boils down to your ability to tolerate the absence of external stimuli. Those with high scores in boredom susceptibility dislike repetition: for example, the same food too many times in a row. They tire easily of the predictable or dull, and they get restless when forced to perform mundane, routine tasks. This last component might be the toughest thing for Olympic athletes who are high-sensation seekers to deal with. In order to be a successful Olympian, you need to spend countless hours practising dull, repetitive workouts and drills.

It's easy to see how all of these aspects of sensation-seeking personalities might exist in Olympic athletes, whether it's a snowboarder experimenting with a daring new trick or an ice hockey forward navigating a puck through a maze of defenders. People with high sensation-seeking personalities in these situations are in their element. Where a low sensation-seeking person might crumble under pressure and give up altogether, they thrive. So, when you're watching the Winter Olympics and wondering how the athletes can handle the pressures and dangers of competition, just remember: For some of them, chaos and intensity are secret weapons of success.

Look at the statements below. Do you think they agree with the claims of the writer in the text? Don't worry about answering Yes, No or Not Given yet.

Write

YES   *if the statement agrees with the claims of the writer*
NO   *if the statement contradicts the claims of the writer*
NOT GIVEN *if it is impossible to say what the writer thinks about this.*

Statements 1–8

1 The skeleton carries a higher level of risk than the bobsled and downhill skiing.
2 Winter Olympic athletes are born with high sensation-seeking personalities.
3 The desire to try new things is part of human nature.
4 High sensation seekers are able to resist and minimise their response to stress.
5 People with high sensation-seeking personalities feel less pleasure when undertaking risky activities.
6 Scientific research on sensation seeking has been carried out since the early twentieth century.
7 Participants in Zuckerman's laboratory study initially displayed similar reactions to sensory deprivation.
8 People with strong disinhibition tendencies act regardless of potential consequences.

1 ▶ How much do you know about Winter Olympics sports? Complete the quiz with the words at the bottom of the page to find out!

Winter Olympics Quiz

1 This sport involves athletes riding down an ice track seated two or four to a sleigh or sled.
....

2 This is a sport where individuals, duos or groups perform on the ice rink.
....

3 In this sport, you lie on your back on a flat sled and race down a specially designed ice track.
....

4 This sport is a two-day event involving both ski jumping and cross-country skiing.
....

5 This sport is a combination of cross-country skiing and target shooting. It is a hugely demanding sport, both physically and mentally.
....

6 This is the sport where athletes race down a track of ice on their stomachs head first.
....

7 This is a black disc made of hard rubber used in ice hockey. It is sometimes referred to as a 'flat ball'.
....

8 This is figure skating's oldest and most difficult jump. The skater needs to generate enough rotational velocity to spin three times while in the air.
....

9 This is a ski race down a winding course marked out by poles.
....

10 This trick involves going upside down twice with three rotations. During training sessions, airbags help cushion the fall until the skateboarder feels ready to attempt the landing on snow.
....

double cork 1080	luge	figure skating	puck	skeleton
slalom	triple axel	Nordic combined	biathlon	bobsled

2 Read the text quickly. <u>Underline</u> SEVEN Winter Olympic sports mentioned in the text.

3 Look again at Exercise 1. Read the first THREE statements in the task carefully and <u>underline</u> the key words in each one. The first one has been done for you.

4 Read Paragraphs 1–3 carefully and the areas of text around the words and phrases you <u>underlined</u> in the statements. Match each statement with an answer. One of the statements is YES and two are NOT GIVEN. Which candidate's answers are correct – Anya or Ben?

Anya: 1 NOT GIVEN; 2 NOT GIVEN; 3 YES

Ben: 1 YES; 2 NOT GIVEN; 3 NOT GIVEN

5 Why might some candidates think that the two NOT GIVEN answers are YES?

6 Read the remaining statements (4–8) and <u>underline</u> the key words and phrases. Next locate these in the text. Then match each statement with an answer.

 **Test facts**

YES / NO / NOT GIVEN

This task tests your ability to decide if statements represent the writer's views. The views will not be stated directly. When you have found part of the text that contains the answer, read every word carefully. For some statements you will need to read the whole text quickly to decide and for others you will only need to read a sentence or two. You should be able to tell from the statement which part of the text to read in order to find the answer.

 **Test task**

7 Do the test practice task. Read the text below and answer Questions 1–9.

A neuroscientist reveals how to think differently

In the last decade a revolution has occurred in the way that scientists think about the brain. We now know that the decisions humans make can be traced to the firing patterns of neurons in specific parts of the brain. These discoveries have led to the field known as 'neuroeconomics', which studies the brain's secrets to success in an economic environment that demands innovation and being able to do things differently from competitors. A brain that can do this is an iconoclastic one. Briefly, an 'iconoclast' is a person who does something that others say can't be done.

This definition implies that iconoclasts are different from other people, but more precisely, it is their brains that are different in two ways: perception and fear response.

Both these functions utilize a different circuit in the brain. The first thing to remember is that the brain suffers from limited resources. It has a fixed energy budget, about the same as a 40-watt light bulb, so it has evolved to work as efficiently as possible. This is where most people are impeded from being an iconoclast. For example, when confronted with information streaming from the eyes, the brain will interpret this information in the quickest way possible. Thus it will draw on both past experience and any other source of information, such as what other people say, to make sense of what it is seeing. This happens all the time. The brain takes shortcuts that work so well we are hardly ever aware of them.

Perception is central to iconoclasm. Iconoclasts see things differently to other people. Their brains do not fall into efficiency pitfalls as much as the average person's brain. Iconoclasts, either because they were born that way or through learning, have found ways to work around the perceptual shortcuts that plague most people. Perception is not something that is hardwired into the brain. It is a learned process, which is both a curse and an opportunity for change. The brain faces the fundamental problem of interpreting physical stimuli from the senses. Everything the brain sees, hears or touches has multiple interpretations. The one that is ultimately chosen is simply the brain's best theory. In technical terms, these conjectures have their basis in the statistical likelihood of one interpretation over another and are heavily influenced by past experience and, importantly for potential iconoclasts, what other people say.

The best way to see things differently to other people is to bombard the brain with things it has never encountered before. Novelty releases the perceptual process from the chains of past experience and forces the brain to make new judgements. Successful iconoclasts have an extraordinary willingness to be exposed to what is fresh and different. Observation of iconoclasts shows that they embrace novelty while most people avoid things that are different.

The problem with novelty, however, is that it tends to trigger the brain's fear system. Fear is a major impediment to thinking like an iconoclast and stops the average person in their tracks. There are many types of fear, but the two that inhibit iconoclastic thinking and people generally find difficult to deal with are 'fear of uncertainty' and 'fear of public ridicule'. These may seem like trivial phobias. But fear of public speaking, which everyone must do from time to time, afflicts one-third of the population. This makes it too common to be considered a mental disorder. It is simply a common variant of human nature, one which iconoclasts do not let inhibit their reactions.

Iconoclasts create new opportunities in every area from artistic expression to technology to business so can be a major asset to any organization. It is crucial for success in any field to understand how the iconoclastic mind works.

Questions 1–9

Do the following statements agree with the claims of the writer in the reading passage?

Write

YES   *if the statement agrees with the claims of the writer*
NO   *if the statement contradicts the claims of the writer*
NOT GIVEN *if it is impossible to say what the writer thinks about this.*

1 Neuroeconomics explores how the brain is linked to achievement in competitive fields.
2 Iconoclasts are distinctive because their brains function differently.
3 Perception is a process we are usually conscious of.
4 Exposure to different events forces the brain to think differently.
5 Iconoclasts are unusually receptive to new experiences.
6 Most people are too shy to try different things.
7 If you think in an iconoclastic way, you can easily overcome fear.
8 When concern about embarrassment matters less, other fears become irrelevant.
9 Fear of public speaking is a psychological illness.

Read quickly through the following text and scan the questions.

Air conditioning

A Ever since our ancestors mastered fire, humans have been able to warm themselves. Cooling down when it is hot has been more challenging. The ancient Egyptians exploited the principle of evaporative cooling to produce ice, which could then be used to cool dwellings. In ancient Babylon, in around 2000 BC, wealthy noblemen would air-condition their homes at night by spraying water onto exposed surfaces – as the water evaporated, it absorbed heat from the house, cooling it. Ancient Indians employed the same principles by hanging wet grass mats on the windward sides of their houses. The Roman emperor Elagabulus sent slaves to bring snow down from the mountains and pile it in his garden, where breezes would carry the cooler air inside.

Nevertheless, this was not something that could be done on a large scale. But in the nineteenth century, entrepreneur Frederic Tudor amassed an unlikely fortune doing something similar in America. He took blocks of ice from frozen New England lakes in winter, insulated them in sawdust, and shipped them to warmer climates for summer. Until artificial ice-making took off, mild New England winters caused panic about an 'ice famine'.

B Air conditioning as we know it began in 1902, but it had nothing to do with human comfort. Willis Carrier, an American engineer at the Buffalo Forge heating and ventilation company was asked to devise a system to control humidity in a Brooklyn printing plant. Printing was an industry plagued by fluctuating humidity and temperature. Fluctuations in heat and moisture caused the printer's paper supply to expand and contract. Even so much as a millimetre was enough to affect carefully aligned coloured inks. As a result, they were not accurately applied to the paper and often smudged.

Carrier developed his system after receiving a flash of inspiration while waiting for a train on a cold, foggy platform. While considering the relationship between temperature and humidity, he formulated principles that he later called his 'Rational Psychrometric Formulae'. His theory enabled him to dry and cool air at the same time to the desired level. His air-conditioning system worked like a fridge by breathing in warm air, passing it across a cold surface and exhaling cool, dry air. Needless to say, the printers were delighted. Buffalo Forge was soon selling Willis Carrier's invention wherever humidity posed problems, such as in flour mills and pharmaceutical factories.

C In 1915, Carrier formed the Carrier Engineering Corporation in order to develop his technology further and his invention started to gain success in non-industrial applications. These included public buildings like theatres. It was an astute choice. Historically, theatres needed to close in summer due to the hot weather. Inside these buildings which lacked windows, human bodies were tightly packed together in tiny seats. And, before electricity, lighting was supplied by flares which added to the heat inside. In the summer of 1880, New York's Madison Square Theatre used four tons of ice a day – an eight-foot fan blew air over the ice and through ducts towards the audience. Unfortunately, though cool, the air was also damp, and with pollution increasing in New England's lakes, the melting ice sometimes released unpleasant smells. The general public first experienced air conditioning in the cinemas of the 1920s. For them it was almost a bigger attraction than the movies themselves – by 1930, over 300 cinemas had installed air-conditioning systems.

D In 1928, Carrier produced its first domestic air-conditioning unit – the 'weather maker'. Business rapidly expanded in the second half of the twentieth century as residential units spread rapidly across America. Cities in the south and southwest once considered nearly impossible to live in during the warm summer months suddenly became very attractive locations in which to live and work. The population of the 'sun belt' – the warmer south of the country from Florida to California – boomed from 28% of Americans to 40%.

E Carrier died in 1950, but his invention has left almost no area of modern life untouched. Climate control enabled the growth of the computer industry, made deep mining for gold, silver and other metals possible, saved valuable manuscripts and paintings for posterity, and kept meat and other produce fresh and cool in supermarkets. Hospitals, schools, airports and office buildings are also maintained at optimum temperature and humidity by air conditioning. Within a century, a system invented to solve a printing problem revolutionised the world.

Read the questions but don't worry about doing this exercise yet.

Questions 1–6

Complete the summary below.

Choose ONE WORD from the text for each answer.

Theatres before the introduction of air conditioning

Before air conditioning was introduced into theatres, they were uncomfortable places for audiences to be in. There were no **1** .... and there was little room between seats.
2 .... provided light which made the buildings even hotter. Theatres were also unable to stay open during the **3** .... because of the hot weather. One theatre used a
4 .... to circulate cool air over ice in an effort lower the temperature inside the building. However, the quality of the air was poor and rather **5** .... odours were emitted on occasion. When air conditioning was installed in the cinemas of the 1920s, it nearly became as much of an **6** .... as the films.

---

1 ▶ How much do you know about air conditioning already? Do the quiz. Compare your answers with a partner.

Air conditioning

1 When was the modern air conditioner invented?

  A 1902 ☐

  B 1922 ☐

2 How many single-room air-conditioning units will there be by 2050?

  A 4.5 billion ☐

  B 6 billion ☐

3 Air conditioners are similar to which other household appliance?

  A dishwashers ☐

  B fridges ☐

4 Air conditioners help .... the air.

  A dehumidify ☐

  B humidify ☐

5 The .... of your home determines your air conditioning needs.

  A size ☐

  B age ☐

6 'Passive' cooling is air conditioning without what?

  A electricity ☐

  B an air-conditioning unit ☐

7 What is a passive-cooling method everyone should try?

  A give everyone in your home a paper fan ☐

  B open the windows on warm days to create air flow ☐

---

2 ▶ Read the text as quickly as you can. In which section (A–E) can you read about

1 how the modern air conditioner came to be invented? ....
2 the growth in popularity of air conditioners for private homes? ....
3 the ways in which air conditioning has transformed all aspects of life? ....
4 how early civilisations tackled the problem of keeping themselves cool? ....
5 the introduction of air-conditioning systems to cinemas? ....

3 ▶ Read the heading of the summary on the previous page. Which section of the text (A–E) do you need to focus on to complete the task? ....

4a ▶ In which questions of the summary (1–6) do you need to look for these parts of speech to complete the gaps?

singular noun   ....

plural noun   ....

adjective   ....

4b ▶ Look at the THREE questions that require a singular noun. For which question do you need to write a word beginning with a vowel? ....

5a ▶ Look at four students' answers for Question 1. Why are they incorrect?

electricity   *window*   air conditioning   *windos*

5b ▶ Complete the summary. Then check your answers in the key.

☑ **Test facts**

Summary completion (without options)

For this task, you need to use exact words from the text to fill the gaps. The gaps may require more than one word and the word or words must fit grammatically. They will not necessarily be used in the same order as they appear in the text.

☑ **Test task**

6 ▶ Do the test practice task. Read the text below and answer Questions 1–4.

Serendipity – accidental discoveries in science

What do photography, dynamite, insulin and artificial sweetener have in common? Serendipity! These discoveries, which have made our everyday living more convenient, were discovered partly by chance. However, Louis Pasteur noted the additional requirement involved in serendipity when he said, '...chance favours only the prepared mind'.

The discovery of modern photography provides an example of serendipity. In 1838, L.J.M. Daguerre was attempting to 'fix' images onto a copper photographic plate. After adding a silver coating to the plate and exposing it to iodine vapour, he found that the photographic image was improved but still very weak. Desperate after an investigation lasting several months, Daguerre placed a lightly exposed photographic plate in the cupboard in which laboratory chemicals such as

alcohol and collodion were stored. To his amazement, when he removed the plate several days later, Daguerre found a strong image on its surface.

This image had been created by chance. It was at this point that Louis Pasteur's 'additional requirement' came into play: Daguerre's training told him that one or more of the chemicals in the cupboard was responsible for intensifying the image. After a break of about two weeks, Daguerre systematically placed new photographic plates in the cupboard, removing one chemical each day. Unpredictably, good photographic images were created even after all chemicals had been removed. Daguerre then noticed some spilt mercury on the cupboard shelf, and he concluded that this must have improved the photographic result. From this discovery came the universal adoption of the silver-mercury process to develop photographs.

Daguerre's serendipitous research effort was rewarded, a year later, with a medal conferred by the French government. Many great scientists have benefited from serendipity, including Nobel Prize winners. In fact, the scientist who established the Nobel Prize was himself blessed by serendipity. In 1861, the Nobel family built a factory in Stockholm to produce nitroglycerine, a colourless and highly explosive oil that had first been prepared by an Italian chemist fifteen years earlier. Nitroglycerine was known to be volatile and unpredictable, often exploding as a result of very small knocks. But the Nobel family believed this new explosive could solve a major problem facing the Swedish State Railways – the need to dig channels and tunnels through mountains so that the developing railway system could expand. However, as turnover increased, so did the number of accidental explosions resulting from the use of nitroglycerine.

According to one version of how the eventual solution was found, a metal container of nitroglycerine sprang a leak, and some of the liquid soaked into packaging material that lay around the container. Nobel immediately set to work to examine the connection between the two materials and found that when the packaging material was mixed with nitroglycerine, it could be pressed into a compact solid. This solid retained the explosive power of the liquid, but was entirely safe and reliable because it would not ignite until set off by a blasting cap. Nobel called his invention 'dynamite'.

As a scientist who had worked systematically towards a solution for a number of years, Nobel immediately understood the importance of his discovery. But the discovery had only come about because of his perseverance. Through Nobel's clear vision, systematic research and his quick grasp of the significance of his discovery, he set himself apart from the many scientists who were not 'fortunate' enough to create new products that would make them famous.

Questions 1–4
Complete the summary below.
Choose NO MORE THAN TWO WORDS from the text for each answer.

Daguerre's experiments

Daguerre's work illustrated the comment made by Louis Pasteur that in order to take full advantage of a lucky discovery, scientists need to have a **1** .... He found that exposure to **2** .... had the desired effect on a silver-coated photographic plate, but only to a very limited extent. To his great surprise the image then became much clearer when it was stored in a cupboard. By a process of elimination, he discovered that neither collodion nor **3** .... were responsible for this improvement. In fact, the removal of all the chemicals did not affect the quality of the image. It was a small amount of **4** .... that had produced the desired effect.

Read quickly through the following text and scan the questions.

Cryodrakon boreas

A A new species of giant pterosaur has been discovered in Alberta, Canada whose icy, windswept lands gave the flying reptile its genus or official name – *Cryodrakon boreas*, meaning 'frozen dragon of the north wind'. Dr David Hone, a paleontologist at Queen Mary University in London and one of the authors of a research study about the new species, remarked, 'It's a stark landscape in winter and we wanted to try and evoke that'.

The *Cryodrakon boreas*, which had the wingspan of a small plane, once soared over the heads of dinosaurs. It lived in what is now western Canada about 76 million years ago, during what is known as the Cretaceous period. Although the fossils were unearthed in frozen, desolate badlands, the area was as warm as the Mediterranean when *Cryodrakon boreas* was alive. Crocodile fossils were also found in this region 'which always rule out very cold temperatures', Hone said.

B The partial skeleton that was identified as *Cryodrakon boreas* was unearthed in 1992, but paleontologists assumed that the remains belonged to a pterosaur called *Quetzalcoatlus northropi*, first described in 1975. This creature had a beak the size of a man and wings over 11 metres wide, making it the largest flying animal ever known.

A couple of key advances prompted paleontologists to re-examine their views on *Quetzalcoatlus*. In recent years they have found more fossils of azhdarchids, a group belonging to the family of pterosaurs. The bones were discovered in parts of Africa, Europe and Central Asia, giving a wider array of shapes and sizes within this pterosaur group. In addition, some researchers have been able to see the *Quetzalcoatlus* fossils up close, including Dr Mike Habib, a paleontologist at the University of Southern California, who measured the bones to model how the creature flew. The model helped them understand not only how the animal soared and dived, but also how it hunted for food.

C As a point of comparison, Habib visited Canada's Royal Tyrrell Museum to see the partial pterosaur skeleton unearthed in 1992. This consisted of part of the neck, legs, shoulder and wing bones of a single young pterosaur. He saw that it had suffered many battle wounds during its lifetime, with scratched bones and the tooth of a velociraptor-like meat-eating dinosaur imbedded in one of the fossils. The creature was more likely to have been scavenged than hunted, as the pterosaur already had a wingspan of about five metres, and the meat eater was likely less than two metres long.

D When Habib was measuring the bones to map how the creature flew, he began to suspect it was not *Quetzalcoatlus* at all. He was able to establish it was an azhdarchid, but the real breakthrough came while studying the animal's neck vertebrae. He discovered that the formation of the pneumatophores, the holes through which air sacs once entered the bone's interior, was unlike that of any other known azhdarchid. The holes were also hollow like bird bones, to make them lighter for flight. Habib and his team realised that these were the bones of an entirely new type of pterosaur.

E *Cryodrakon* would have been as tall as a giraffe, with a similarly long neck and legs on a short body, it could weigh up to 250 kilograms and had wings that stretched about 10 metres from tip to tip. In addition to flight, which it used in order to ecape danger or to seize its prey, the creature would have walked and run on all fours, most likely with a giraffe-like gait – moving both legs on one side at the same time to avoid tripping.

The animal had no chewing apparatus and would probably have eaten whatever would fit in its mouth, including baby dinosaurs, lizards and mammals. 'Imagine a "giant flying murder head" about 3.5 times the length of its body', or "a pair of wings that carry round a big head for guzzling things"', Habib said. It still had its predators though – it would have been prey for large predators such as tyrannosaurs and crocodiles.

F More work on *Cryodrakon* may help add more clues to this large pterosaur's anatomy and lifestyle. Hone and Habib plan to investigate the internal structure of its humerus, corresponding to the human upper arm bone, to see where the bone was strongest. This should, in turn, yield insights on how the animal walked, took flight and landed. Another paleontologist, Taissa Rodrigues at the Federal University of Espirito Santo in Brazil, is interested in studying thin sections of *Cryodrakon* bones in order to find out how the pterosaur grew from hatchling to adult. Future fossils could even test whether male and female *Cryodrakon* varied in size. 'It's amazing,' she says, 'just to see how far we're going'.

Read the list of headings but don't worry about matching them to the paragraphs yet.

List of Headings	
i A species less diverse than previously believed	....
ii An animal inhabiting a very different climate from nowadays	....
iii Evidence of physical conflict revealed in remains	....
iv Two important developments challenge a long-held view	....
v Conflicting theories about how the creature flew	....
vi More secrets about the animal yet to be uncovered	....
vii One unique arrangement leads to formal identification	....
viii A creature with a physique designed for effective hunting	....

1 **Read the text as quickly as you can and complete the fact file. The information is given in the order of the text.**

Fact file: Cryodrakon

Genus (official name): *Cryodrakon boreas*

Country found: **1** ....

Meaning of name: **2** .... *of the north wind*

When it lived: **3** .... *years ago*

Family: *Pterosaur*

Group: *Azhdarchidae*

Height: *similar to that of a* **4** ....

Weight: **5** .... *kg*

Wingspan: *approximately* **6** .... *metres*

Diet: *small dinosaurs,* **7** ...., **8** ....

Predators: *tyrannosaurs,* **9** ....

2a **Look at the <u>underlined</u> sentence in Section A and read the list of headings at the top of this page. Which one seems to be the most likely heading?** ....

2b **Read Section A in full and check your answer. <u>Underline</u> evidence from Section A which supports the heading.**

3 Look at the student's notes about the main ideas in Sections B–D of the text at the start of Worksheet 4. Put the correct letter (B–D) next to the notes.

1 Special features of neck bones distinguish Cryodrakon from other pterosaurs. ....

2 Marks on bones show Cryodrakon did a lot of fighting when alive. ....

3 The true identity of Cryodrakon remains unclear for a long time. ....

4 Write your own notes about the main ideas for Sections E and F of the text. Then discuss your ideas with a partner and compare them with the suggestions in the answer key.

....

....

5 Compare ALL the notes for Sections B–F with the list of headings i–viii above Exercise 1. Are any of the main ideas similar to the headings? ....

6 Match the words and phrases 1–8 from the headings with the words and phrases of similar meaning a–h.

1 inhabiting	a battle
2 physical conflict	b await discovery
3 important developments	c fossils
4 unique	d living in
5 yet to be uncovered	e not as varied as
6 remains	f body
7 less diverse than	g key advances
8 physique	h unlike any other

7 Read the text at the start carefully and match the headings i–viii above Exercise 1 with Sections A–F. You do not need them all.

 **Test facts**

Matching headings to paragraphs/sections

This task requires you to choose headings that correctly summarise either individual paragraphs or sections consisting of more than one paragraph. Sometimes it is possible to find one sentence that conveys the main idea – this could be at the beginning, the middle or at the end of a paragraph or section. But often the main idea can only be understood by reading the paragraph or section in full.

☑ *Test task*

8 ▶ Do the test practice task. Read the text below and answer Questions 1–4.

The Little Ice Age

A This book will provide a detailed examination of the Little Ice Age and other climatic shifts, but first let me provide a historical context. We tend to think of climate – as opposed to weather – as something unchanging, yet humanity has been at the mercy of climate change for its entire existence, with at least eight glacial episodes in the past 730,000 years. Our ancestors adapted to the universal but irregular global warming after the end of the last great Ice Age, around 10,000 years ago, with dazzling opportunism. They developed strategies for surviving harsh drought cycles and decades of heavy rainfall or unaccustomed cold; they adopted agriculture and stock-raising, and founded the world's first pre-industrial civilisations in Egypt, Mesopotamia and the Americas. But the price of sudden climate change, in famine, disease and suffering was high.

B The Little Ice Age lasted from roughly 1300 until the middle of the nineteenth century. Only two centuries ago, Europe experienced a cycle of bitterly cold winters; mountain glaciers in the Swiss Alps were the lowest in recorded memory and pack ice surrounded Iceland for much of the year. The climatic events of the Little Ice Age did more than help shape the modern world. They are the deeply important context for the current unprecedented global warming. The Little Ice Age was far from a deep freeze, however; rather an irregular seesaw of rapid climatic shifts, few lasting more than a quarter-century, driven by complex and still little-understood interactions between the atmosphere and the ocean. The seesaw brought cycles of intensely cold winters

and easterly winds, then switched abruptly to years of heavy spring and early summer rains, mild winters, and frequent Atlantic storms, or to periods of droughts, light winds and summer heat waves.

C Reconstructing the climate changes of the past is extremely difficult, because systematic weather observations only began a few centuries ago, in Europe and North America. Records from India and tropical Africa are even more recent. For the time before records began, we have only 'proxy records' reconstructed largely from tree rings and ice cores, supplemented by a few incomplete written accounts. We now have hundreds of tree-ring records from throughout the northern hemisphere, and many from south of the equator too, amplified with a growing body of temperature data from ice cores drilled in Antartica, the Peruvian Andes, and other locations. We are close to a knowledge of annual summer and winter temperature variations over much of the northern hemisphere going back 600 years.

D This book is a narrative history of climatic shifts during the past ten centuries, and details how people in Europe adapted to them. Part One describes the Medieval Warm Period, roughly 900 to 1200. During these three centuries, Norse voyagers from Northern Europe explored northern seas and visited North America. It was not a time of uniform warmth, for then, as always since the Great Ice Age, there were constant shifts in rainfall and temperature. Mean European temperatures were about the same as today, perhaps slightly cooler.

Questions 1–4

The reading passage has four paragraphs, A–D.

Choose the correct heading for each paragraph from the list of headings below.

Write the correct number i–vi next to the Questions 1–4.

List of Headings	
i Predicting climate changes	**1** Paragraph A ....
ii The relevance of the Little Ice Age today	**2** Paragraph B ....
iii Ways in which people have responded to climate change over time	**3** Paragraph C ....
iv A study covering a thousand years	**4** Paragraph D ....
v How past climatic conditions can be determined	
vi A growing need for weather records	

Describing trends

1 Read the task and look at the pie charts. Then answer the questions.

> *The three pie charts below show the annual spending by one UK school in 2000, 2010 and 2020.*
>
> *Summarise the information by selecting and reporting the main features and make comparisons where relevant.*
>
> *Write at least 150 words.*

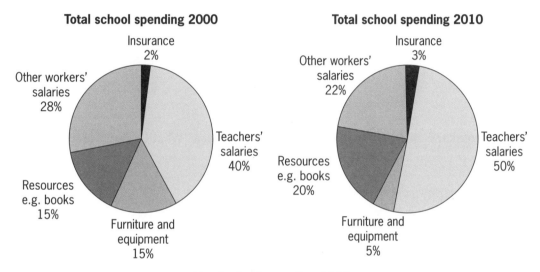

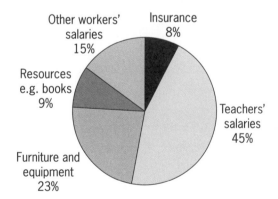

1 What was the largest percentage spent on in all three years?

2 What was the smallest percentage spent on in all three years?

3 Did the percentage spent on insurance go up or down between 2000 and 2020?

4 Was there a big or a small change in the percentage spent on furniture and equipment between 2010 and 2020?

5 Was there a considerable or a slight difference between the percentage spent on insurance and resources in 2020?

6 Was there a significant or a small decrease in percentage spent on resources between 2010 and 2020?

Describing numbers

In your summary, it is important to use a range of language to describe numbers, for example, phrases, fractions and percentages.

2 Match the five percentages (1–5) from the pie charts with the descriptions (a–e).

1 2%	**a** a fifth
2 9%	**b** half
3 20%	**c** nearly a quarter
4 23%	**d** almost a tenth
5 50%	**e** a tiny proportion

3 Look at the notes the student has made about the pie charts. What do they refer to? Choose the correct words from the box. Write them in the gaps.

Furniture and equipment	Insurance	Other workers' salaries
Resources	Teachers' salaries	

1 .... amounted to half of total spending in 2010.

2 .... saw an upward trend, growing from a tiny proportion to 8% by 2020.

3 .... decreased to only 5% of total expenditure in 2010.

4 .... declined significantly from 28% in 2000 to only 15% of spending in 2020.

5 .... fell dramatically from a fifth of total expenditure in 2010 to only 9% by the end of the period.

4 Look again at the notes in Exercise 3. Find the words and phrases with the following meanings. There is an example to help you.

1 went down (three verbs)   *decreased* ....

2 a big change (two adverbs)   ....

3 a rising movement (a noun phrase)   ....

 Get it right!

Find the mistakes in the sentences and correct them.

1 The amount spent on insurance went up slight between in 2000 and 2010.

2 There was a considerably increase in the amount of money spent on furniture.

5 Sentences 1 and 2 below were written by two different students. Are they from the introduction or the overview of their answers? ....

> **1** The pie charts illustrate how much one UK school spent on different running costs in three separate years – 2000, 2010 and 2020.

> **2** The three pie charts show the changes in annual spending by a particular UK school in 2000, 2010 and 2020.

6 Which sentence is better? 1 or 2? Why? ....

....

7 Now write your own introduction for the task in Exercise 1.

....

....

Making comparisons

8 It is important to be able to compare the information in the pie charts. Use the information to help you complete the sentences. Use some of the words and phrases in the box.

slightly more	slightly less	much/far more	much/far less
least	most	compared to/with	broadly/largely the same

1 In all three years, ... of the school's expenditure was on staff pay.

2 The .... amount was spent on insurance in all three years.

3 Expenditure on other workers' salaries and resources in 2010 was ....

4 .... money was spent on insurance in 2000 than 2010.

5 In 2020, ... money went on furniture and equipment .... resources.

9 Write the rest of your answer for the task in Exercise 1.

....

....

....

....

....

10 Complete the checklist after you have finished writing.

Have you ...

- used synonyms in your introduction? ☐
- used past simple verbs throughout? ☐
- made comparisons? ☐

- used adverbs such as 'significantly'? ☐
- included some phrases to describe numbers? ☐

 **Test task**

11 Now do the test practice task. Read the text in the box and write your answer.

> *The first pie chart below shows how energy is used in an average Australian household. The second chart shows the greenhouse gas emissions that result from this energy use.*
>
> *Summarise the information by selecting and reporting the main features, and make comparisons where relevant.*
>
> *Write at least 150 words.*

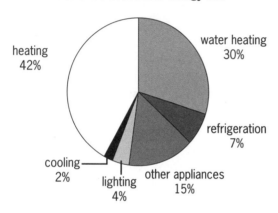

Australian household energy use

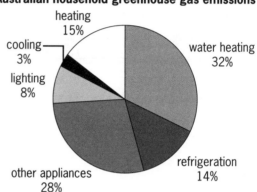

Australian household greenhouse gas emissions

....
....
....
....
....
....
....
....
....
....
....
....
....
....
....
....

Describing a process

1 ⟩ **Read the task and look at the diagram below.**

> The diagrams below show the life cycle of a species of large fish called the salmon.
>
> Summarise the information by selecting and reporting the main features and make comparisons where relevant.
>
> Write at least 150 words.

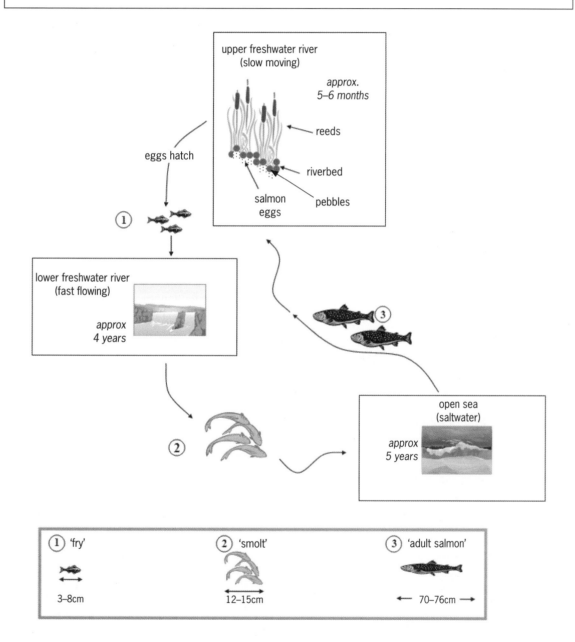

Are the following statements true or false? Write T for True or F for False next to each one.

1 The life cycle of the salmon consists of several physical stages. ....

2 The entire life of a salmon is spent in a freshwater environment. ....

3 The maximum length of a mature salmon is 70 centimetres. ....

2 ▶ Some key words that you need to write your summary will be given in the diagram. Read the descriptions and match them to the words in the diagram. Write the words at the end of each sentence.

1 This word describes living in water that is not the sea and is not salty. ....

2 This is the term for a very small fish, which measures no more than eight centimetres. ....

3 This word means to come out of an egg. ....

4 These are tall plants with a hollow stem that are found in or near water. ....

5 This is the area of ground over which a river usually flows. ....

6 This describes the water which is found in an open sea environment. ....

7 This term is used to describe a juvenile salmon. It can measure up to 15 centimetres in length. ....

8 These are smooth, round stones which are found in or near water. ....

> ### *Present simple passive*

We use the present simple passive to describe a process – when we are more interested in what happens than who does something.

- <u>We call</u> salmon 'fry' when they measure between 3 and 8 centimetres in length. (**Active**: 'We' meaning 'people' is not important here. We are more interested in the length of the salmon.)
- Salmon <u>are called</u> 'fry' when they measure between 3 and 8 centimetres in length. (**Passive**: 'are called' avoids referring to any people unlike in the Active and is more formal. The Passive goes straight to the information of the salmon's length.)

3 ▶ Look back at the sentences in Exercise 2. Which FOUR sentences contain passive forms of the verb? The first one has been done for you.

...4... ....

4 ▶ Read part of the student's answer to the task in Exercise 1. The answer attained a score of 4.5 for grammatical range and accuracy. Which part of the life cycle is the candidate mainly focusing on? The early stage or the later stage of the life cycle? How do you know?

> When salmon fry reach a length of between twelve and fifteen centimetres, they are then call 'smolt', and at this stages of their lives they are migrate further downriver into the open sea. After five years on sea the salmon will have grown to adult size. They then begins swimming back to their place of birth which they will lay their eggs.

....

....

....

Grammatical range and accuracy

The marking criteria includes grammatical range and accuracy. A key aspect of this includes using grammatical structures correctly.

5a **Look at part of the student's answer in Exercise 4 again and <u>underline</u>**

1 ONE error with the passive form of the verb.
2 ONE error with the active form of the verb.
3 ONE error with the singular/plural form of a noun.
4 ONE error with the present simple tense.
5 ONE error with a preposition.
6 ONE error with a relative clause.

5b **Correct the errors and then check your answers in the key.**

 *Test tips*

It is important to include an overview of the whole process in either the opening paragraph or the final paragraph.

The overview should:
- give general information about the type of process.
- say how many stages there are.
- consist of between one and three sentences.

6a **Read the student's overview. Does it come from the opening or final paragraph of their answer? How do you know?**

> In summary, the diagrams show how the salmon passes through four distinct physical stages. This involves hatching out of an egg, growing into fry and then smolt before becoming an adult salmon. In the first three stages of its life, the fish inhabits a freshwater environment in slow moving and then fast moving rivers while the final stage of its lifecycle is spent in salt water.

....

6b **Does the student follow all the instructions for writing an overview? Yes or No?** ....

7a **Now write your own answer to the question in Exercise 1. Compare your answer with the one suggested in the key.**

....
....
....
....
....
....
....

☑ **Test task**

8 ⟩ Now do the test practice task. Read the text in the box and write your answer.

> *The diagrams below show the stages and equipment used in the cement-making process and how cement is used to produce concrete for building purposes.*
>
> *Summarise the information by selecting and reporting the main features and make comparisons where relevant.*
>
> **Write at least 150 words.**

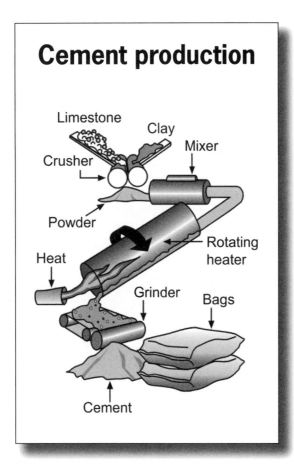

Cement production

Limestone
Clay
Mixer
Crusher
Powder
Rotating heater
Heat
Grinder
Bags
Cement

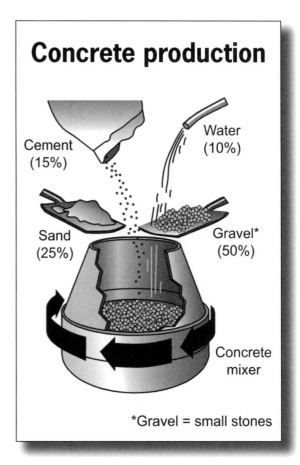

Concrete production

Cement (15%)
Water (10%)
Sand (25%)
Gravel* (50%)
Concrete mixer

*Gravel = small stones

Discussion essay

1a Read the descriptions of three unusual museums and match them to the pictures. Ignore the gaps for now.

A

B

C

1 The instant noodles museum in Osaka, Japan features **a** .... that give information about the history of instant noodles. The museum even has a special tunnel that visitors can walk through to see packages of instant noodles from all over the world. You can also play some **b** .... games, one of which includes designing packaging for your own cup of noodles to take away as a **c** .... of your visit.

2 Leila's hair museum in Missouri, USA has a **d** .... of more than 2,000 pieces of **e** .... made from human hair. These include rings, necklaces and earrings. There are also samples of hair from famous people **f** ....

3 The Cancun Underwater Museum in Mexico can be found deep in the Caribbean Sea so it is only **g** .... to certified divers. There are more than 500 **h** .... human figures, vehicles and buildings. Each **i** .... is made from special concrete that helps coral and algae to grow around it. The aim of the museum is to highlight the importance of **j** .... marine life.

1b Complete the descriptions of the museums with the words in the box.

accessible	collection	exhibits	interactive	jewellery
life-size	on display	preserving	sculpture	souvenir

2a Read the following task.

> *In many countries people pay an admission fee to enter museums. Some people believe that it is reasonable for museums to charge admission fees to visitors. Others believe that museums should be completely free of charge and that visitors should not have to pay to enter.*
>
> *Discuss both these views and give your own opinion.*
>
> *Write at least 250 words.*

2b What do you have to do? Tick (✓) A or B?

A Select one of the views to focus on and explain why you agree. ☐

B Make some notes about the two views and give your own view. ☐

3   **Make notes for the task in Exercise 2 below. There is an example to help you.**

First view: museums need money to pay their staff

....

Second view: ....

....

My view: ....

....

4a   **Look at the points the student has made about admission fees for museums. Do they mention any of your ideas?**

1 <u>There is no doubt that</u> museums are expensive places to run. ....

2 <u>It is important to take into account that</u> some people live far from museums so they have travel costs to consider as well. ....

3 <u>It is impossible to argue with the fact that</u> museums need to keep acquiring new exhibits. ....

4 <u>Some people think that</u> charges could deter poorer people from visiting. ....

5 <u>It is important to remember that</u> people already pay for other entertainment and leisure activities. ....

4b   **Which of the points could be used to support the first view and which could be used to support the second view? Put 1 or 2 next to each one.**

5   **Look at the <u>underlined</u> phrases in Exercise 4a. Most of them can be used to introduce the views you agree with. Which ONE phrase can be used to introduce views of people you don't agree with?** ....

6b   **Look back at the notes you made in Exercise 3. Write sentences saying why you agree or disagree with each point you made.**

....

....

....

....

....

☑ *Test tips*

In order to write a well-developed argument, you need to include main points and information which supports each point.

7 Match the student's points 1–5 in Exercise 4a with the supporting information A–E below. Write 1–5 at the end of each statement.

Supporting information

A They have to buy tickets to watch films at the cinema or enjoy performances at the theatre, for example. ....

B It is important for them to attract visitors by adding paintings, sculptures and manuscripts to their collections. ....

C As well as those on low incomes, large families and school groups may also be unable to afford to go to museums if they are expected to pay. ....

D Some visitors may have to travel very long distances in order to visit a museum. They may be deterred from doing so if they have to pay an admission charge in addition to the cost of their journey. ....

E In order to operate at all, museums need revenue so that they can pay the salaries of their staff. Their employees include guides and specialist curators who help to preserve the exhibits. ....

8a Read Paragraphs 2 and 3 of the student's answer below. Ignore the gaps for now.

1 .... admission charges may prevent large families from going to museums. However, many museums already offer discounts for big groups and young children are admitted free of charge. Furthermore, there are museums that allow free entry on one day of each week. For example, in my city, they are free for visitors every Monday.

2 .... museums are far from cheap places to run. They have to pay their staff as well as meet the costs of heating, lighting and security. It seems reasonable that visitors who enjoy looking at the exhibits on display should contribute to these expenses.

3 .... people pay to enjoy many other leisure activities like going to football matches and concerts. Surely, they should be prepared to pay to enter a museum as well.

4 .... museums need to stay relevant and continue to appeal to a wide range of people and age groups. In order to do this, they need to invest in fun, educational interactive displays and facilities like cafes and shops. Without revenue generated by admission fees, they will not be able to keep the museum up to date and interesting.

8b Answer the questions.

1 Which view does the writer agree with in the task – the first view or the second view?

....

....

2 Which ideas in Exercise 4a does the writer mention?

....

....

3 Does the writer consider the other view?

....

....

....

4 Does the writer give an example from their own experience?

....

....

8c Complete the gaps in the text with the phrases (A–D).

A Furthermore, it is impossible to argue against the fact that

B However, there is no doubt that

C Finally, it is important to remember that

D Some people argue that

9 Write your own Paragraphs 2 and 3. Use the phrases in Exercise 8c to help you structure your answer. You can use some of the ideas in Exercise 4a to help you.

....

....

....

....

....

....

....

....

10a Look at the two plans (A and B) for writing an introduction and a conclusion.

A	B
Paragraph 1 (Introduction)	Paragraph 1 (Introduction)
Opinion	General introduction (no opinion)
Paragraph 4 (conclusion)	Paragraph 4 (Conclusion)
Restate opinion	Opinion given for the first time

10b **Read the student's paragraphs. Which plan does the student follow? A or B?**

Paragraph 1

Many people enjoy visiting museums in their leisure time to admire the amazing exhibits on display – from dinosaur bones to unusual sculptures. Some people take the view that museums should be free to all visitors, while others think that it is fair for museums to impose an entry fee. I firmly believe that admission charges are a good thing. ....

Paragraph 4

All in all, I strongly believe that it is fair for museums to charge people for admission. These important centres of learning play a valuable part in preserving our history and need revenue from visitors to keep their collections exciting and accessible to all. ....

11 **Choose ONE of the plans (A or B) in Exercise 10a to follow. Write your own introduction and conclusion.**

 **Test task**

12 Now do the test practice task. Present a written argument or case to an educated reader with no specialist knowledge on the following topic.

> *Some people believe that trips to places such as museums and art galleries should be a compulsory part of high school programmes. Others say that students should complete all their learning within the classroom.*
>
> *Discuss both these views and give your own opinion.*

Give reasons for your answer and include any relevant examples from your own knowledge or experience. Write at least 250 words.

....

....

....

....

....

....

....

....

....

....

....

....

....

....

....

....

....

....

....

....

....

....

....

....

Advantages and disadvantages

1a **Read the following task.**

> ***Nowadays, more and more people are choosing to use electronic readers or 'e-readers' instead of printed books.***
>
> ***Do the advantages of this development outweigh the disadvantages?***
>
> **Give reasons for your answer and include any relevant examples from your own experience.**
>
> **Write at least 250 words.**

1b **What are the advantages and disadvantages of e-readers? Make notes below. There is an example to help you.**

Advantages: light and easy to carry around ....

....

....

Disadvantages: ....

....

....

2a **Read the three short texts about e-readers as quickly as you can.**

A **The Caxton**

One good thing about this e-reader is it's waterproof. In other words, you can enjoy your favourite novel in the bath without worrying! Another benefit is it looks good – it's made from aluminium and comes in a range of striking colours. It even feels like a book. For instance, you can turn the pages in the same way as you would with a real book. The only downside is that it's not the lightest e-reader available so it's not that easy to hold one-handed.

B **Scribe**

The best thing about this e-reader is that there's enough room on it to store as many as 1,500 books – so if you're not enjoying one book, you can always just move on to another. However, one drawback is that the battery drains down quickly so you have to wait as it charges up again before you can continue reading! One other issue is that the screen is quite small so you may have to take regular breaks to avoid straining your eyes.

C **Verdana**

What's not to love about this e-reader? One advantage is that it's as light as a feather and so slim that it will fit neatly into your pocket. Another good point is that its screen can change colour so that you can read comfortably at any time of day or night. You can even use it when you're wearing sunglasses! One final benefit is that it can survive for at least an hour in a metre of water without getting damaged. Basically, this e-reader tops the lot!

© Cambridge University Press and Assessment 2022

2b **Where does each text come from?**

an essay .... a review .... a personal letter ....

3a **Which text A, B or C is the most positive about e-readers?**

....

3b **Are any of <u>your</u> ideas mentioned in the reviews in Exercise 2a?**

4 **Read the reviews again. Which review or reviews mention the following features?**
Write A, B or C in the gaps.

1 storage ....

2 appearance ....

3 weight ....

4 battery ....

5 size of screen ....

6 screen brightness ....

7 how waterproof it is ....

5a **Choose the correct paraphrases for the phrases from the texts.**

1 One good thing about
 A One advantage of ☐ **B** One drawback of ☐

2 Another benefit is
 A One further issue is ☐ **B** One further argument on the plus side ☐

3 For instance
 A For example ☐ **B** In other words ☐

4 The only downside is
 A The one drawback is ☐ **B** Another negative aspect is ☐

6 **Look at the words and phrases used to talk about advantages and disadvantages. <u>Underline</u>**
ONE word or phrase in each group that has a different meaning.

Advantages: benefit	drawback	good thing	positive aspect
Disadvantages: issue	negative aspect	on the downside	on the plus side

7a Read paragraphs 2 and 3 of the student's answer below. Ignore the gaps for now. Which of <u>your</u> ideas do they mention?

One of the best things about e-readers is that they are much more portable compared to printed books. **a** ...., they can be carried about very easily and slipped into a bag. **b** ...., I can download as many books as I want onto my e-reader before going on holiday – there is no need to pack heavy, bulky books in my luggage. **c** ...., unlike printed books, many e-readers are waterproof so you do not have to worry if you accidentally drop your device in the sea. **d** .... is that you can download e-books very cheaply and sometimes even one chapter of a book for free. **e** ...., I have often been able to read a sample of an e-book before buying it.

However, there are some disadvantages to e-readers. **f** .... some people may find it uncomfortable to read a book on a screen for long periods. However, there are devices available which enable you to adjust the size of the words and the brightness of the screen. **g** .... that you do not have the tactile nature of paper and the pleasure of holding a physical book in your hand. However, there are some e-readers that provide a flipping animation. **h** .... I have an app on my device that enables me to experience the sound and sight of the page turning in front of me on the screen.

7b Choose the correct answers to the questions.

1 What best describes the student's overall opinion about e-readers?

positive ☐   **negative** ☐

2 Does the student think that the advantages of e-readers outweigh the disadvantages?

yes ☐   **no** ☐

3 The student repeats the words 'advantages' and 'disadvantages' throughout the text.

true ☐   **false** ☐

7c Complete the gaps in the student's text with suitable phrases from the reviews in Exercise 3. There may be more than one suitable answer for some of the gaps.

☑ Test facts

Advantages and disadvantages essay

The words used in this kind of question can vary. For example, you may have to answer one of these questions:

- Do the advantages of X outweigh the disadvantages?
- What are the advantages and disadvantages of X?
- Do you think that X is a positive or a negative development?

---

8 Read the tips below for writing a conclusion. Then read the two conclusions to the essay. Which conclusion follows both tips?

> ☑ **Test tips**
>
> • Briefly summarise what you have said in the body of your essay.
> • State your own position on the question.

A On balance, I believe that the benefits of e-readers outweigh the drawbacks. We live in an ever-changing world and the ability to read wherever and whenever we want offers a great deal of convenience. I am convinced that e-readers are a positive development – not only do they make our lives easier, but they are better for the environment too – by not using up valuable paper resources and taking up less space!

B In conclusion, there are many advantages and disadvantages to e-readers. They are very convenient to carry around and they can be cheaper in the long run compared with printed books. However, it is important to remember that there are drawbacks too. People can suffer eye strain when using them to read.

9a Write your own answer to the task in Exercise 1. You can continue writing on the next page.

....
....
....
....
....
....
....
....
....
....
....
....
....
....
....
....
....
....

....
....
....
....
....
....
....
....
....
....
....

9b **Look at your completed answer. Complete the checklist.**

Have you ...

- included information from your own experience? ☐
- used phrases to give examples for your points? ☐
- introduced a contrasting view that looks at the other side of the argument? ☐
- given your opinion in the conclusion? ☐

9c **Compare your answer with the suggested answer in the key.**

 **Test task**

10 Now do the test practice task. Read the text in the box and write your answer.

> *Nowadays more and more people are choosing to listen to audio books instead of reading printed books and e-readers.*
>
> *Do the advantages of this development outweigh the disadvantages?*

Give reasons for your answer and include any relevant examples from your own experience. Write at least 250 words.

....
....
....
....
....
....
....
....
....
....
....
....
....
....
....
....
....
....
....
....
....
....
....
....
....

Double question essay

1 Read the following task.

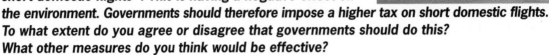

> *Nowadays an increasing number of people are taking short domestic flights*. This is having a negative effect on the environment. Governments should therefore impose a higher tax on short domestic flights. To what extent do you agree or disagree that governments should do this? What other measures do you think would be effective?*
>
> Give reasons for your answer and include any relevant examples from your own knowledge or experience.
>
> Write at least 250 words.
>
> ** travelling short distances by plane within their own country*

What idea are you being asked to agree or disagree with? ....

....

2 Do the quiz. Match the definitions on the topic of the environment with the phrases in the box.

Environment Word Quiz

Definitions

1 This describes residents taking holidays within their own country, for example, Britons who holiday in Cornwall. ....

2 This means the same as renewable energy, which comes from natural resources rather than non-renewable sources. These sources cause less harm to the natural environment. ....

3 This involves having as little impact as possible on the environment when making a journey. For example, this may involve choosing to travel by rail instead of air. ....

4 This describes toxic substances, for example, harmful gases or chemicals deposited into the atmosphere. They can have a severe negative impact on the local environment, and in large quantities, on a global scale. ....

5 This refers to policies, laws, services or products that have a minimal or reduced impact on the environment. ....

6 This is a type of fuel used in trains, buses and other vehicles. ....

7 This is the increase in world temperatures caused by polluting gas. ....

8 This involves buying carbon credits, giving money to help fund projects such as planting trees or investing in renewable energy. These projects aim to reduce the amount of carbon emissions by a measurable amount. ....

9 This describes the large amount of greenhouse gas (including carbon dioxide and methane) which is generated by human activities. Ways of reducing this include using public transport and consuming food that doesn't require much transportation. ....

air pollution	diesel fuel	domestic tourism	eco-friendly	global warming
green energy	large carbon footprint	offsetting your emissions		sustainable travel

3 Look at the words and phrases in Exercise 2 again. Group them under the two headings below. There is an example to help you.

Good for the environment	Bad for the environment
	diesel

4a Read the student's introduction to the first question in the task.

> There is no doubt that more and more travellers are choosing to take domestic flights these days which is seriously affecting the environment. This is because individual short trips can have a remarkably large carbon footprint. However, despite the high carbon emissions produced by planes, I firmly believe that tackling the problem of global warming needs far more than a simple tax to make people reconsider how they travel.

4b What best describes their view?

A strong agreement ☐　　**B** partial agreement ☐　　**C** strong disagreement ☐

5 Look at the points below. Which points support agreement and which support disagreement? Put A for Agreement or D for Disagreement next to each one.

1 Trains produce fewer carbon emissions than planes. ....

2 Taxing flights would be especially unfair for people who live in a remote area ... .

3 The taxes could provide extra revenue for the government ... .

4 Higher taxes might provide an incentive for airlines to produce more fuel-efficient planes ... .

5 It is not right to limit people's personal freedom to travel in the way they want. ....

6 ▶ **Match the points 1–5 in Exercise 5 with the endings A–E below. Write 1–5 at the end of each statement.**

A … <u>but</u> this money would not necessarily be used to tackle the very serious problem of air pollution. ....

B <u>Nevertheless</u>, I do understand those who say that restricting an individual's freedom of choice is a small price to pay and that immediate action is needed. ....

C <u>However</u>, it is important to remember that they are not a source of clean energy either. ....

D … <u>although</u> there is likely to be resistance from some companies. ....

E … <u>despite</u> the seriousness of the problem of emissions caused by internal flights within a country. ....

7 ▶ **Write the correct linking words from Exercise 6 in the spaces below to complete the rules.**

1 _____

It can be used to introduce a contrasting idea.

It can go at the beginning of a sentence or in the middle.

It is followed by a noun.

2 _____ _____

It is used to contrast two ideas in the same sentence.

It can go at the beginning of a sentence or in the middle.

If it goes at the beginning of a sentence, there is a comma in the middle.

3 _____

It is used to contrast two ideas in the same sentence.

It goes in the middle of the sentence.

4 _____ _____

It is used to contrast ideas in two different sentences.

It usually goes at the beginning of the second sentence.

It is immediately followed by a comma.

◎ Get it right!

Read the student's sentences. Correct them by using different linking words.

1 Despite fewer flights would mean more trains, this could place pressure on the rail network.

2 Travelling by rail or bus may take longer than flying however you get to see more of the country than you would by sitting on a plane.

---

8   Which of the points in Exercise 5 do you agree and disagree with? Can you add your own ideas? Make notes below.

....

....

....

....

....

9a   Read part of the student's answer to the task. Ignore the <u>underlined</u> words for now. Which of the main ideas in Exercise 5 and YOUR ideas do they mention?

> There is no doubt that an increasing number of people are choosing to take domestic flights these days and this is having a serious impact on the environment. This is because these individual short trips can have a remarkably large carbon footprint. However, <u>despite / although</u> the high carbon emissions produced by planes, I strongly believe that tackling the problem of global warming is likely to need more than a simple tax.
>
> <u>Although / Despite</u> there can be no doubt that short flights are a huge source of carbon emissions, imposing a tax is unlikely to discourage people from flying short distances – particularly those who live in remote areas and have no other option but to fly. In my country, for example, people have no choice <u>however / but</u> to travel from islands to the mainland by air because the journey by boat takes too much time. Furthermore, it is sometimes the case that it is cheaper to fly than to use other forms of transport such as the train or the car. <u>Nevertheless / Although</u>, there are various other measures that could be implemented to reduce carbon emissions.

....

9b   Choose the correct <u>underlined</u> linking words to complete the candidate's answer. You can look back at the rules for the use of linking words in Exercise 7.

10   Look again at the second question in the task: 'What other measures do you think would be effective?' Make notes about your ideas. There is an example to help you.

<u>Build more railway tracks so that people can travel by train instead.</u> ....

....

....

....

....

11 ▸ **Read the student's answer to the second question in the task. Which THREE measures do they suggest? Are any of your ideas mentioned?**

> Nevertheless, there are various other measures that could be implemented that would have a huge effect on reducing greenhouse gas emissions. Firstly, governments could persuade airlines to design planes which have more efficient engines and use cleaner fuels. Furthermore, there needs to be more investment in improving bus and rail services and ensuring that these run efficiently and that the infrastructure is maintained. This would make people far more willing to consider travelling between cities by bus or train. Finally, I think that there is a need for more education about the effects of global warming and how cutting back on air travel could have a positive impact. For example, some people simply do not realise just how polluting short flights are.

....

....

....

12a ▸ **Write your own answer to the task. When you have finished, complete the checklist.**

....

....

....

....

....

....

....

....

....

....

....

....

....

....

....

....

....

....

Have you …

- given your opinion in the first paragraph? ☐
- considered both sides of the argument? ☐
- used examples to support your points? ☐
- included some linking expressions? ☐
- answered the second question? ☐
- restated your opinion in the final paragraph? ☐

12b **Compare your answer to the suggested answer in the key.**

☑ *Test task*

13 **Now do the test practice task. Read the text in the box and write your answer.**

Increasing the price of petrol is the best way to solve growing traffic and pollution problems in towns and cities.

To what extent do you agree or disagree with this opinion?

What other measures do you think might be effective?

Give reasons for your answer and include any relevant examples from your own knowledge or experience. Write at least 250 words.

....

....

....

....

....

....

....

....

....

....

....

....

....

....

....

....

Friends and family

1 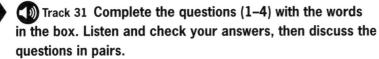 Track 31 **Complete the questions (1–4) with the words in the box. Listen and check your answers, then discuss the questions in pairs.**

alike	like	like doing	look like

1 Are you and your friends ....?

2 What are your family ....?

3 What do you and your friends .... together?

4 Who, in your family, do you .... most?

2 〈🔊〉 Track 32 **Match the questions (1–4) from Exercise 1 to the appropriate answers (A–D). Then listen and check your answers.**

A It depends on the weather really. If it's nice, we love chilling out in the park. It helps us relax after a hard day at college.

B Well, mum's tall and elegant and quite strict – especially about things like keeping my room tidy, or when I want to stay out late with my mates.

C That'll be my dad. Our features are very similar; for example, we've got the same chin and nose.

D I'm like my best friend Martha. We're both quite impatient and when it comes to sports, we're very competitive as we hate losing.

3 **Put a cross next to the things you should NOT say if you don't hear the examiner when they ask you a question.**

1 What? ☐

2 Pardon? ☐

3 Sorry? ☐

4 Repeat? ☐

4 〈🔊〉 Track 33 **Put the words into the correct order to complete a suitable two-sentence response when you don't hear what the examiner has said. The first sentence has been done for you. Then listen and check your answers.**

1 please you could again it say
'I didn't quite catch that. .... Could you say it again please ....?'

2 question repeat you could the
'Sorry, I missed that. ....?'

3 mind you saying again that would please
'I couldn't quite hear you. ....?'

5 🔊 Track 34 **Listen to four students answering Part 1 questions. Decide which statement (1–4) applies to which candidate (A–D).**

1 The student's answer is too short and the examiner needs to ask a follow-up question. ....

2 The student's answer is too long and goes off topic. ....

3 The student's answer is clearly a prepared speech. ....

4 The student's answer is full and sounds natural. ....

6 **Put the words and phrases into the correct columns.**

| as | due to | for instance | including | like |
| since | such as | this happens because | | |

Words and phrases to give examples	Words and phrases to give reasons

7 **Think about how you would answer these questions. Then match the questions to the answer pairs (A–G).**

1 Do you often go out with your family at the weekends? (Why/Why not?)

A No, there isn't. / Yes, there is.

2 Have you always liked the same type of family holidays? (Why/Why not?)

B No, I don't. / Yes, I do.

3 Would you like to move, with your family, to another town or city? (Why/Why not?)

C No, I wouldn't. / Yes, I would.

4 Are there any sports you dislike playing? (Why/Why not?)

D No, I didn't. / Yes, I did.

5 Is there anything you did with your family in the past, that you don't do now? (Why/Why not?)

E No, I haven't. / Yes, I have.

6 Did you enjoy making friends when you first started school? (Why/Why not?)

F No, there wasn't. / Yes, there was.

7 Was there anything you disliked about school? (Why/Why not?)

G No, there aren't. / Yes, there are.

8 🔊 Track 35 **Listen to Laya answering the questions about sports fully and naturally. As you listen, make a note of the examples and reasons she gives. Also, which question does Laya not completely answer?**

1 Do you enjoy playing sports?

2 Is there any sport you would like to try in the future?

3 Do you often watch sport on TV?

4 What sports do children normally do at school in your country?

Notes

....

....

....

....

....

....

....

....

9 **Answer the questions in Exercise 8 yourself. Give full answers which include reasons and examples. If possible, record yourself answering the questions. Listen to your recording and check your answers against the questions (1–6) below. If you cannot record yourself, consider asking a friend to listen to you.**

1 Did I use suitable words or phrases to give examples? ☐

2 Did I use suitable words or phrases to give reasons? ☐

3 Did I give full answers? ☐

4 Were my answers too short? ☐

5 Were my answers too long? ☐

6 Did I move away from the topic? ☐

☑ *Test facts*

Worksheet 1 provides practice for Part 1 of the Speaking test. Part 1 will last about five minutes. The examiner will ask you questions about yourself and about other familiar topics, such as your family, your hometown or your likes and dislikes.

☑ *Test tips*

- You will not be penalised if you ask the examiner to repeat the question, as long as you don't keep doing it; however, make sure you know the correct way to ask them to repeat something.

- In Part 1 of the Speaking test, it is important to answer the examiner's questions fully and naturally. This means you should support yes/no answers with a reason or an example and avoid giving answers you have learnt from a prepared speech.

Descriptions

1 🔊 **Track 36 Listen to two students called Changying and Abbas talking about Part 2 of the IELTS Speaking test and answer the questions. You can listen more than once.**

1 What is Changying concerned about?

   A speaking without the examiner asking questions

   B speaking for up to two minutes

2 What revision strategy do Changying and Abbas disagree about?

   A Learning a wide range of grammar is as important as fluency.

   B Learning complete answers is useful.

3 How does Changying intend to improve her pronunciation?

   A by listening to native English speakers

   B by listening to examples of her own speaking practice

4 Why does Abbas think Changying should time herself speaking?

   A so she can practise speaking for the right amount of time

   B so she can check she's answered the question fully

5 Why does Changying agree it's better not to make up stories?

   A You will sound more confident.

   B You can give more details.

2 🔊 **Track 37 Look at the task and then listen to Changying giving her talk. As you listen, complete Changying's sentences (1–5).**

> **Describe a shop in your town or city that you sometimes use.**
>
> **You should say:**
>
>   **what sorts of products or service it sells**
>
>   **what type of people go there**
>
>   **where it is located**
>
> **and explain why you like going to this shop.**

1 You .... a local shop I go to every so often.

2 So, ..., I'm going to talk a shop called New From Old.

3 I think the .... go there are ...

4 .... location, it's not far from where I live.

5 What .... why I like shopping in New From Old?

3 🔊 Track 37 **Changying uses linking language (e.g.** *because of, due to, for example*) **to expand her ideas, and pronouns and determiners (e.g.** *she, he, they, it, that, this*) **to avoid repetition. Listen again and put the phrases in the order you hear them. There is one you do not need.**

A it's people like her who tend to go there ....

B but it's more than that ....

C like my Aunt Miriam, for example ....

D stuff like that ....

E so that's why I go there ....

F they repair it ....

G as I said ....

H when I say … I mean ....

4 **Look at the task and the two sets of notes (A and B). Think about which style of notes you would be most comfortable using and why.**

> **Describe something you have seen that you would really like to own.**
>   **what the thing is**
>   **how long you have wanted to own it**
>   **where you first saw it**
> **and explain why you would like to own it.**

A

> How long have I wanted one?
> • not entirely sure
> • early childhood (around 5)

> Where did I first see it?
> bedtime story books

> What do I want in the future?
> a horse

> Why do I want to own one?
> • riding: takes skill and courage
> • feelings: thrilling yet relaxing.
> • fitness: time outdoors / fresh air

B

What: Video Game – New World

How long: Since it came out last year

Where: Can't quite remember. Could have been Akane's house / gaming competition

Why: Special effects / thrilling / all my mates have it

---

5 🔊 Track 38 **Listen to Abbas answering the question in Exercise 4. As you listen, write down the notes Abbas may have made before he started speaking. You can use any style of note taking you prefer, (e.g. a list, mind map or diagram).**

Test task

6 Look at the task. Spend a minute making notes. Then use your notes to talk for one to two minutes. If you can, record yourself speaking so that you can listen after and think about how you can improve. If not, ask a friend to listen to you. Remember to use different points in the question to help you structure your talk and connect and expand your ideas with linking phrases and pronouns.

> Describe someone you know who does something well.
> You should say:
>   who this person is
>   how you know them
>   what they do well
> and explain why you think this person is so good at doing this.

 Test facts

In Speaking Part 2, you will be asked to talk about a specific topic. You will be given one minute to prepare before talking for between one and two minutes. You may be asked to describe a person, time, place or experience. You may also be asked to describe your feelings.

 Test tips

Two of the criteria that you are assessed on are coherence and fluency. Coherence means how well you organise your ideas so the listener can follow what you are saying. Using the different points in the task to structure your talk might help you to be more coherent.

Discussion topics

A

should children ? which learn skills at school

B

skills ? home should any are there at learn they which

C

which be and important skills the future ? will in abilities

1 Put the words into the correct order to make questions. More than one option may be possible.

A .... ?

B .... ?

C .... ?

2 🔊 Track 39 **Look at the techniques for developing ideas then listen to Berdine answering the questions in Exercise 1. Tick (✓) the techniques she uses.**

Techniques for developing ideas

1 giving your own point of view or opinion ☐

2 giving others' points of view or ideas ☐

3 suggesting a solution to a problem ☐

4 explaining why something happens ☐

5 offering a contrasting idea ☐

6 making future predictions ☐

7 discussing advantages and/or disadvantages of something ☐

8 giving examples to support ideas ☐

9 giving factual information ☐

3 🔊 Track 39 **Listen again and complete what Berdine says with the words you hear. You can listen more than once.**

1 It .... that children ...

2 One way .... this is to teach life skills.

3 Let's take socialising ....

4 .... they don't know how to properly socialise ...

5 Well, ... that life skills ...

6 For .... they may have no siblings ...

7 .... I think children should learn ...

8 I think we're .... skills related to that.

9 Technology offers us, and the planet, ...

4 ▶ **Write the techniques from Exercise 2 next to the most appropriate phrases.**

1 some might suggest ....

2 the drawbacks are significant ....

3 things like that ....

4 one way of approaching this ....

5 as far as I'm concerned ....

6 it's unlikely that ....

7 as opposed to ....

8 it's a known fact that ....

9 this is due to ....

5 ▶ **Put the sentences into the correct categories in the table.**

1 That depends on the situation.

2 I'm not so sure about that.

3 I think we need to consider both sides.

4 My thoughts exactly.

5 That's not the way I see it.

6 There's no doubt about it.

Disagree	Neither disagree nor agree	Agree

6 🔊 Track 40 **In Part 3 Advik is asked about the topic of work and money. Look at one of the questions he was asked. Then, listen to Advik and answer the questions (1–3).**

EXAMINER: Some people say it would be better for society if everyone got the same salary. What do you think about that?

1 How far does Advik agree with the opinion in the question?

....

2 What phrase does he use to express his view?

....

3 What examples does he give to support his ideas?

....

....

....

....

☑ *Test task*

7 **Look at the questions and spend a minute deciding how you might answer them. Then answer the questions using the prompts to help you, if you wish. If possible, record yourself so you can listen afterwards and think about how you can improve. If not, ask a friend to listen to you and give you feedback. Remember to develop your ideas with reasons, examples, and solutions.**

Owning things

1 What types of things do young people in your country want to own nowadays?

2 Do you think television can make people want to own more things?

3 What should people do with things they no longer want?

4 Some people think owning things is a sign of success. Do you agree?

5 Would life be better if nobody owned private property?

Answer prompts:

Unlike in the past, …

As I see it …

One possibility might be to …

We could overcome this by …

I think we need to consider both sides …

It's highly likely that …

◎ Get it right!

If you are asked to give your opinion about the views of other people, or to talk about people generally, it is important that you do not talk only about yourself, friends or family as you did in Part 1. Look at the Part 3 question and then decide which is the best response (1–3).

EXAMINER: Do you think people will consider that having lots of possessions is a sign of success in the future?

RAJ (1): Well, I don't believe that having a lot of possessions will necessarily equal success in the future. For me, being successful will be about having a happy and healthy family rather than the number of items I own.

MARIA (2): Not really, no. I think the focus on having good mental health will continue and for many, success will be more about living a stress-free life, for example, less work and more family time, than buying flash cars.

HANU (3): Absolutely. My dad really wants to own a premium car, like a Lamborghini, in the future. He thinks it will show other people how successful he is. I'd like lots of expensive possessions in the future too.

 **Listening Worksheet 1: Answering multiple-choice questions**

Read the sentences and choose the correct options.

1 Questions will appear *in a random order / in the order you hear them*.

2 When answering questions *don't choose / choose* an option because it includes the same word you hear.

3 *Word matching / Listening for paraphrases* will usually help you select the correct option.

4 Look for options which express *the same idea / a different idea* as the speaker but in *the same way / a different way*.

5 You *will / won't* hear information about options other than the correct one.

6 *More than one / Only one* option will be correct for each question.

7 You will hear the Listening text *once / twice*.

8 Questions may focus on the ideas and opinions of the *speaker / listener*.

 **Listening Worksheet 2: Answering matching questions**

Read the statements. Are they TRUE or FALSE?

1 The speakers may contradict and correct each other. ....

2 Before you listen, it's a good idea to try to paraphrase the words in the options. ....

3 Paraphrases will not include opposites. For example, these opposites, *rather boring* instead of *not very interesting*. ....

4 Questions sometimes follow the order you hear them. ....

5 You know when questions are coming as they are clearly signposted in the text. ....

6 If you miss a question, spend time trying to answer it before moving on. ....

7 You will need to use all the options. ....

8 After listening, it's a good idea to use the remaining options to answer any questions you have missed. ....

Think about it — Listening Worksheet 3: Flowchart completion

Match the sentence starters (1–8) with the endings (a–h) to make sentences about flowchart completion.

1 In flowchart completion, you must use a word or words from the Listening text	**a** ideas and move between topics.
2 Typically, the flowchart will show the order	**b** a question in each stage.
3 You may not need to answer	**c** needed for each gap.
4 Use the headings and subheadings on the question paper	**d** by connecting sentences with arrows.
5 Think about the type of word	**e** the order of the text you hear about them.
6 Signposting may be used to connect	**f** will not be the same as the words you hear.
7 The questions will follow	**g** to help you follow the speaker(s).
8 The words around the gap	**h** to complete the gaps.

Think about it — Listening Worksheet 4: Labelling

Complete the sentences with the words from the box. Use each word once only.

compass	directions	letters	location	monologue	orientate	question	tourist

For map labelling, you will hear a **1** .... You may be asked to follow
2 .... so it's important to familiarise yourself with language of movement and
3 .... Maps may be of a part of a town or **4** .... destination.
As you listen, write down the correct letter next to the **5** .... The questions
follow the order of the Listening text and there may be **6** .... that you do not need
to use. If you are given a **7** .... icon, it is likely you will hear phrases like 'to the
east'. Use these phrases to help **8** .... yourself as you listen.

 **Think about it** Listening Worksheet 5: Table completion

Read the statements about table completion. Are they TRUE or FALSE?

1 Before you listen, you should use the headings to predict the type of word you need. ....

2 If the instructions say **write ONE word** and your answer contains TWO words, it might be correct. ....

3 If the answer is a plural noun form and you write down a singular noun form, you will not be penalised. ....

4 Asking yourself questions using the information either side of the gaps may develop your understanding and help you hear the correct answer. ....

5 Table-completion questions will only appear in Part 1 and Part 2 of the Listening test. ....

6 You may be asked to choose the correct answer from a number of options. ....

7 You should avoid making simple mistakes by reading the instructions carefully. ....

8 You should check your answers before transferring them to the answer sheet. ....

 **Think about it** Listening Worksheet 6: Note completion

Read the sentences and choose the correct options.

1 Before you listen, look at the questions and think about what paraphrases you *might hear / might not hear*.

2 Identifying synonyms and paraphrases will help you 'hear' when the *incorrect answer / correct answer* is coming.

3 Don't leave any question *answered / unanswered*.

4 *Guess / Don't guess* any answers you are not sure about.

5 You will need to listen for *specific / general* information.

6 Write down *a similar / the exact* word that you hear.

7 *Use / Don't use* the headings to help you follow the speaker.

8 The questions *follow / may not follow* the order of the text you hear about them.

 **Think about it**   **Reading Worksheet 1: Multiple-choice questions**

Complete the sentences with the words from the box. Use each word once only.

idea	options	phrase	reading	section	text	underline	words

For this type of task, it is a good idea to start by **1** .... the whole text quickly to

get an overall **2** .... of what the text is about. Write down a

3 .... that describes the topic area of each paragraph or **4** ....

as this may help you answer the questions later. You will be given a set of **5** ....

for each question and you need to select the correct one. Scan the questions and

6 .... the key words in the options. Think about synonyms and different ways to

express the **7** .... that you have underlined as these will be referred to in the

8 .... Read the relevant section of the text and options carefully before choosing

your answer.

 **Think about it**   **Reading Worksheet 2: YES, NO, NOT GIVEN questions**

Read the statements. Are they TRUE or FALSE?

1 YES, NO, NOT GIVEN questions are the same as TRUE, FALSE, NOT GIVEN questions. ....

2 YES, NO, NOT GIVEN questions test your ability to understand a writer's views or claims. ....

3 The writer's views are always stated directly. ....

4 For each statement you will need to read one or two sentences only. ....

5 YES statements contradict the claims of the writer. ....

6 For NOT GIVEN statements, it is impossible to say what the writer thinks about something.

....

7 There will always be more YES than NO answers. ....

8 The relevant part of the text will be clearly signposted in the statement. ....

....

 **Think about it** Reading Worksheet 3: Summary completion

Read the sentences and choose the correct options.

1 For summary completion questions, you *may / will* never be given options.

2 For questions without options, you must use *the exact / a similar* word from the text.

3 You *can / must* not go over the word limit given in the question.

4 The word or words you write down *don't have to / have to* fit grammatically.

5 The words *will / may not* follow the order of the text.

6 Read the words before and after the gap to work out the *type of word / number of words* you are looking for.

7 It's a good idea to read the text quickly *after / before* you scan the questions.

8 Summary completion usually comes from *one section / the whole* of the text.

 **Think about it** Reading Worksheet 4: Matching headings

Match the sentence starters (1–8) with the endings (a–h) to make sentences matching headings.

1 You are given a list of headings	**a** understand main ideas or distinguish them from supporting ideas.
2 There will always be more headings	**b** which you must match to paragraphs or sections.
3 Some headings	**c** to fully understand the main idea.
4 You may find a heading has	**d** will not be used.
5 The list of headings will not	**e** be found in one sentence.
6 The main idea may	**f** follow the order of the text.
7 Often, however, you must read the whole paragraph	**g** already been matched as an example.
8 This task is designed to test your ability to	**h** than paragraphs or sections

Think about it — Writing Worksheet 1: Writing Task 1

Read the sentences and choose the correct options.

1 In Writing Part 1, you *will / will not* be given a graph, table, chart or diagram to describe.

2 You should aim to spend around *20 / 40* minutes on this task.

3 Your response should be written in *an informal / a formal style*.

4 You *must / must not add* your own ideas.

5 You should write a minimum of *250 / 150* words.

6 It is important *to make / not to make* comparisons about the information presented.

7 Select *the main features / all the features* to summarise.

8 If you write *too few / too many* words, you will probably lose marks.

Think about it — Writing Worksheet 2: Describing a process

Complete the sentences with the words from the box. Use each word once only.

academic	describe	information	overview	paragraph	sentences	stages	well-organised

In Writing Part 1, you may be asked to **1** .... a process. When writing about a process, it is important to include an **2** .... in the opening or closing **3** .... Your overview should include general **4** .... about the type of process presented, together with the number of **5** .... included the process. Overviews do not need to be long; around one to three **6** .... is ideal. Make sure your overview is **7** .... and uses **8** .... language accurately.

 **Think about it** Writing Worksheet 3: Discussion essay

Read the sentences. Are they TRUE or FALSE?

1 You do not need to do Writing Part 2 if you have already completed Writing Part 1. ....

2 You should read the task carefully and make sure you include all the points mentioned. ....

3 Write your essay in an informal and friendly style. ....

4 Aim to write no more than 150 words. ....

5 Your answer should include reasons for your views. ....

6 Your ideas and views should be supported with examples. ....

7 Your essay does not need to include a conclusion. ....

8 Use a range of formal language and grammatical structures. ....

 **Think about it** Writing Worksheet 4: Advantages and disadvantages

Match the sentence starters (1–8) with the correct endings (a–h).

1 The words used in this type	**a** is a negative or positive development.
2 You may have to discuss whether	**b** of task can vary.
3 You could be asked if a situation	**c** the main points in the body of your essay.
4 Your conclusion should summarise	**d** on the question.
5 You should state your position	**e** experiences to support your views.
6 Remember to introduce contrasting	**f** views that consider the other side of the argument.
7 Include information from your own	**g** 'on balance' or 'in conclusion'.
8 Summarise your points with phrases like	**h** disadvantages outweigh advantages.

 **Think about it** Writing Worksheet 5: Double question essay

Read the sentences and choose the correct options.

1 There are *one / two* parts to this type of question.

2 You *must / don't have* to answer both parts.

3 You can gain higher marks in coherence and cohesion by using a wider range of *linking words / opinions*.

4 *despite / nevertheless* can be used to contrast two ideas in the same sentence.

5 You *will / will not* be penalised if your answer goes off topic.

6 It is *important / not important* to use a range of vocabulary and grammatical structures accurately.

7 You *don't have / do have* to have an opinion on the question.

8 Organise your writing into clear *notes / paragraphs*.

 **Think about it** Speaking Worksheet 1: Speaking Part 1

Complete the text about Speaking Part 1 with the words from the box. Use each word once only.

correct	dislikes	familiar	five	naturally	penalised	reasons	repeat

In Speaking Part 1, the examiner will ask you questions about **1** .... topics such as your family, friends, hometown or your likes and **2** .... You should try and answer the questions fully and **3** .... , which means that you should give examples and **4** .... to support YES/NO answers. If you ask the examiner to **5** .... the question, you won't be **6** .... ; however, make sure you know the **7** .... way to ask the examiner to say something again and don't do it too often. This part of the test lasts about **8** .... minutes.

Match the sentence starters (1–8) with the correct endings (a–h) to make sentences about Speaking Part 2.

1 In Part 2, you will be asked to	**a** prepare what you want to say.
2 You will have one minute to	**b** can follow what you are saying.
3 You should aim to talk for	**c** the examiner will ask you one or two follow-up questions.
4 You might be asked to describe an	**d** you to be more coherent.
5 When you have finished your talk,	**e** between one and two minutes.
6 Two criteria you are assessed on are	**f** coherence and fluency.
7 Organise your ideas so the listener	**g** talk about a specific topic.
8 Using the task structure may help	**h** experience, place or person.

 **Think about it** Speaking Worksheet 3: Speaking Part 3

Read the statements about Speaking Part 3. Are they TRUE or FALSE?

1 If the question includes an opinion, you should always agree with it. ....

2 If you are asked about people generally, you should not talk about yourself. ....

3 The Part 3 interview lasts around two to three minutes. ....

4 Giving short YES/NO answers is acceptable. ....

5 You could develop your ideas by offering solutions to problems. ....

6 In Part 3, you should avoid giving factual information. ....

7 One technique for developing ideas is to discuss the advantages or disadvantages of something. ....

8 You can use the phrase 'some might suggest' to present an opinion. ....

Listening Worksheet 1

The underlining indicates where in the track the answers come from.

1

See underlining in Track 1.   1A   2A   3B

NARRATOR: 🔊 **Track 1**
Listening Worksheet 1

TRUST MANAGER: Welcome to the Dolphin Conservation Trust and thank you for agreeing to support our charity by working here as volunteers. Before I go through this week's activities, there are a few facts about dolphins I'd like to share with you. First their teeth. As you know, we use ours to bite and chew what we eat, don't we? You might think that's the same for dolphins, but in fact they <u>use theirs for catching what they eat</u>. Then there's sleeping. Did you know that dolphins sleep with half their brain awake and in low levels of alertness? <u>If they didn't do this, they would stop breathing</u>. They can continue swimming while sleeping as well, though digestion has to wait until later. Finally, although their rubbery skin repairs itself quickly, did you know that it damages easily? In fact, it can <u>tear or break from the softest touch</u> on any solid surface.

2

1 'Humans' The speaker says 'we' use ours to bite and chew which refers to humans and not dolphins.

2 'Digestion' The speaker says dolphins can 'continue swimming while sleeping … though digestion has to wait until later', which means digestion does not happen until the dolphin is awake.

3 'Hard' The speaker mentions 'softest' which might have led you to circle 'soft'; however, the speaker says that their skin 'tears or breaks from the softest touch on any solid surface', not that the surfaces are soft.

3

See underlining in Track 2.   C

NARRATOR: 🔊 **Track 2**
Listening Worksheet 1

TRUST MANAGER: Right, now I want to tell you about this week's programme. Today is Wednesday and you were going to go to the indoor aquarium, but that project doesn't start until next week, so you

---

have the rest of the day to relax. Tomorrow, you're off to the sea life hospital where researchers are examining changes in a dolphin's heart rate when they interact with people. Here you will help feed and care for our sick dolphin, Molly. Then, <u>on Friday</u>, you're at the education centre where you'll have the opportunity to <u>assist our part-time biologist with a study</u> that's measuring the amount of carbon dioxide dolphins exhale after they swim. It will be a fantastic experience.

4

1 **project** is a word match for the word 'project' in the question and for incorrect option A.

2 **researchers** is a word match for the word 'research' in the question and for incorrect option B.

4 **help** is a word match for the word 'help' in the question and for incorrect option B.

5

See underlining in Track 3.

NARRATOR: 🔊 **Track 3**
Listening Worksheet 1

NARRATOR: 1

TRUST MANAGER: As a sea life charity, it is our <u>purpose to protect</u> all living marine animals.

NARRATOR: 2

TRUST MANAGER: We simply must <u>ensure people have a better understanding of impacts</u> that coastal erosion has on sea turtles.

NARRATOR: 3

TRUST MANAGER: During their week at the Trust, schoolchildren will <u>participate in various activities</u>.

NARRATOR: 4

TRUST MANAGER: You may not know this, but <u>80% of our budget is spent</u> on funding our ocean emergency project.

6a

It used to be <u>controversial</u> among local <u>experts</u>, but thankfully that's been resolved.

6b

Although the speaker says, 'controversial among local experts' which is a paraphrase for A: Experts do not agree, the speaker also says, 'used to' and 'has been resolved'. So although experts did not agree in the past, they do agree now. Also, as A is written using the present tense, it cannot be the correct option.

7

See underlining in Track 4.

1 B is correct as the speaker says, 'It will also be helpful for studies we have planned' which is a paraphrase for 'helping future research'. D is incorrect. The words 'expensive' and 'critical' connect with 'Money' and 'urgently' but the speaker says expensive equipment is not needed.

2 D is correct because the speaker says, 'It's not a quick process' which is a paraphrase for 'takes … a long time'. The word 'technology' in the text is a word match for C but 'out of date' in the text means the opposite of 'new'.

3 C is correct because 'the latest specialist equipment' is a paraphrase for 'uses new technology'. A is incorrect. Although 'controversial among local experts' is a paraphrase for 'Experts do not agree'. The speaker also says, 'used to' and 'has been resolved' so, experts did not agree.

4 F is correct because the speaker says it is popular and specifically among volunteers (unpaid workers).

NARRATOR: **Track 4**
Listening Worksheet 1

TRUST MANAGER: Right, before we finish, I want to briefly mention four of our conservation projects: turtle monitoring; cave mapping; reef surveying and beach clear. OK so, turtle monitoring can be fascinating. It doesn't need expensive equipment and we have already collected some critical data about population numbers. It will also be helpful for studies that we have planned for the future about how the marine life in the area is changing. With cave mapping, we are creating accurate and detailed maps of the local underwater system. It's not a quick process, especially as some of our technology is a little out of date, but it's worthwhile, nevertheless. Next, there's reef surveying. It used to be controversial among local experts, but thankfully that's been resolved. Most surveys are done by divers using the latest specialist equipment to determine the health of the coral ecosystem. Finally, we have beach cleaning. You'd think it would take ages – we've ten miles of beach to clear of plastic and litter which marine mammals can get caught in – but its popularity among our volunteers means that isn't the case.

---

8 Test task

See underlining in Track 5.

1 and 2

C and E are correct. C is correct because Hannah says, 'The charity uses its money to support campaigns – for example, for changes in fishing policy and so forth.' 'Uses its money to support' is a synonym for 'helps finance'. E is correct because Hannah says, 'volunteers working in observation, office work and other things' which is a synonym for 'help in various ways'.

A is incorrect because children make up '35%' of the membership which is not 'most'.

B is incorrect because the Trust is 'still fairly small compared with the big players'.

D is incorrect because the Trust 'hopes soon to be able to employ its first full-time biologist'. 'hopes soon' refers to a future intention not a present fact.

3

B is correct because Hannah says, 'it has made our activities even more widely publicised and understood'. 'our activities' is a synonym for 'work'.

A is incorrect because although Hannah refers to 'an enormous amount of money' which is a paraphrase for 'extra money', she uses 'not' to show the opposite is the case: the award did **not** bring in extra money.

C is incorrect because Hannah says it may **not** 'bring in extra members' although they hope it will.

4

A is correct because exploration creates 'a lot of noise' which is a synonym for 'sound'.

B is incorrect because Hannah says, 'there'll be little [not very much] pollution'.

C is incorrect because there is 'very little [not very much] water traffic' and although 'companies want to increase exploration', Hannah does not say anything about the movement of ships.

5

B is correct because Hannah talks about a book that she could not put down.

A is incorrect because Hannah says she had 'never seen one'. The word 'home' in the option could mislead as it is a word match for 'dolphins leaving their home' in the text.

C is incorrect because Hannah says nothing about anyone speaking at school. The word 'school' in the option could mislead as it is a word match for 'I hadn't been … interested in them at school' in the text.

6 D is correct because Hannah says that Moondancer has been 'rather elusive since January' and has not 'been sighted'. C is incorrect because although 'most active' has a similar meaning to 'energetic'. Hannah says '**not** the most active' which has the opposite meaning.

7 B is correct because Echo has been 'captured …
on film hundreds of times' which is a synonym for
'photographed frequently'. 'A real character as she
seems to adore', may have led you to 'loving' in A;
however, 'adore' (love) refers to Echo wanting her photo
taken and not to her personality.

8 F is correct because Kiwi's 'particularly large fin on
her back' is a synonym for 'unusual shape'. 'The latest
from the scheme' may have made you consider E;
however, the text refers to giving birth and not to joining
the scheme.

9 C is correct because 'leaping out of the water with
great enthusiasm' is a synonym for 'very energetic'.
Hannah says 'I can picture him doing it now' which
may have led you to B; however, she is referring to
having the image of Samson in her mind, not to taking
photographs.

NARRATOR: 🔊 **Track 5**
Listening Worksheet 1

INTERVIEWER: Today we're pleased to have on
the show Hannah Wells from the
Dolphin Conservation Trust. Tell us
about the Trust, Hannah.

HANNAH: Well, obviously its purpose is to
protect dolphins in seas all around
the world. It tries to raise people's
awareness of the problems these
marine creatures are suffering
because of pollution and other
threats. It started ten years ago
and it's one of the fastest growing
animal charities in the country –
although it's still fairly small
compared with the big players in
animal protection. We are
particularly proud of the work we do
in education – last year we visited a
huge number of schools in different
parts of the country, going round to
talk to children and young people
aged from five to eighteen. In fact,
about thirty-five per cent of our
members are children.
The charity uses its money to
support campaigns – for example,
for changes in fishing policy and so
forth. It hopes soon to be able to
employ its first full-time biologist –
with dolphin expertise – to monitor
populations. Of course, many
people give their services on a
voluntary basis, and we now have
volunteers working in observation,
office work and other things.

INTERVIEWER: And I believe you've recently won an
award?

HANNAH: Yes, we were really pleased to
win the award from the Charity
Commission last year – for our
work in education. Although it's
not meant an enormous amount
of money for us, it has made
our activities even more widely
publicised and understood. In the
longer term it may not bring in extra
members but we're hoping it'll have
this effect.

INTERVIEWER: Is it possible to see dolphins in UK
waters? I've heard you can see them
in Scotland.

HANNAH: Yes, we have a big project there.
This has long been a haven for
dolphins because it has very
little water traffic. However,
that may be about to change
soon because companies want
to increase exploration there.
We're campaigning against this
because, although there'll be little
pollution, exploration creates a lot
of underwater noise. It means the
dolphins can't rest and socialise.
This is how I became interested
in dolphin conservation in the first
place. I had never seen one and I
hadn't been particularly interested in
them at school. Then I came across
this story about a family of dolphins
who had to leave their home in
the Moray Firth because of the oil
companies and about a child who
campaigned to save them. I couldn't
put the book down – I was hooked.

INTERVIEWER: I'm sure our listeners will want
to find out what they can do to
help. You mentioned the 'Adopt a
Dolphin' scheme. Can you tell us
about that?

HANNAH: Of course! People can choose
one of our dolphins to sponsor.
They receive a picture of it and
news updates. I'd like to tell you
about four which are currently
being adopted by our members:
Moondancer, Echo, Kiwi and
Samson and they are all individual.
First there's Moondancer, not the
most active of the group, he's been

---

rather elusive since January and hasn't yet been sighted by our observers, but we remain optimistic that he'll be out there soon. Then there's Echo who's our real 'character' as she seems to adore coming up close for the cameras and we've captured her on film hundreds of times. Next, we have Kiwi. The latest from the scheme to give give birth – she's quite shy and came to us after she got caught up in a fishing net. Easily identified by the particularly large fin on her back. Finally, there's Samson – he jumps really high – quite surprisingly so for his age and size really – our youngest member, although almost the longest. Anyway, he's always leaping out of the water with great enthusiasm. I can picture him doing it now. Yes, they're all very different.

INTERVIEWER: Well, they sound a fascinating group …

Listening Worksheet 2

1

1 B
2 C (Distance learning is when you do not attend university, school or college, but study from where you live.)
3 A

2

3 The speaker wants to discuss a work placement.

NARRATOR: 🔊 Track 6
Listening Worksheet 2

MAN: Hi Jess, could we catch up on a video call next week? As you know, I'll have finished my second year soon, and I'm thinking about getting some experience in an office. I could really do with your advice …

3

See underlining in Track 7.

1 choose one that's fun
2 make plans for after graduation
3 prove you know the topic in detail
4 don't get lazy
5 ask for some support

NARRATOR: 🔊 Track 7
Listening Worksheet 2

WOMAN: Hmm, advice about your work placement … Right … first make sure that you choose one that's fun. There's no point spending a year doing something that you …
Next, remember it's not about what you are studying now. You need to make plans for after graduation. What I'd suggest is …
Well, in order to be selected, you must prove you know the topic in detail. There is a lot of competition, and they might choose …
I'm sure you know this already, but whatever you do, don't get lazy. The company reports back to college, and you don't want …
Well, It's a really big decision, so before you decide, you might want to ask for some support. I'm sure your tutor will be able to help you …

4

1 in the second year of the course
2 when first choosing where to go
3 when sending your choices
4 when writing your personal statement
5 when doing the year abroad

5

Mia is referring to Question 3. She says, 'send your choices in' which is a signpost for 'sending your choices'.

NARRATOR: 🔊 Track 8
Listening Worksheet 2

MIA: Then about six months before you go, you have to send your choices in.

6

See underlining in Track 9.

1 B is the correct answer. Although the speakers say 'places', which might be connected to the word 'travel' in A, Mia tells Josh that students need to get 'good marks' and know the subject well, which are paraphrases for 'show ability in' the subject (Theatre Studies). You know the answer is coming when Mia says, 'second year' (see bold text in Track 9).

NARRATOR: 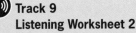 **Track 9**
Listening Worksheet 2

JOSH: Hi Mia, I wanted to ask you about the year abroad option. Would you recommend doing that?

MIA: Yes, definitely. It's a fantastic chance to study in another country for a year.

JOSH: I think I'd like to do it, but it looks very competitive – there's only a limited number of places.

MIA: Yes, so next year when you are in the **second year** of the course, you need to work really hard in all your theatre studies modules. <u>Only students with good marks get places – you have to prove that you know your subject really well.</u>

7a

Possible paraphrase ideas:

A   reserve flights and accommodation

C   be punctual / not be late

D   obtain written references

E   organise the last year of study

F   ensure it's the right course for you

G   get assistance

7b

See underlining in Track 10 for the position of the answers and bold text for signposting.

1   B (See Exercise 6)

2   F is correct. Mia talks about 'a programme that would fit in with what I wanted' and then gives course examples to support this idea. This is a paraphrase for 'making sure the course's focus is relevant' in the option.

3   C is correct. Mia talks about 'missing the deadline' and 'getting a move on', which refer to 'being on time' in the option. The word 'friend' in the listening may have drawn you to G 'ask for help'; however, Mia does not mention 'friend' in this context.

4   G is correct. Josh says he will get 'final-year students to give me some tips', which is a way of saying he will 'ask them for help'. The words 'read what they wrote' may have drawn you to D 'letter of recommendation'; however, the context of a recommendation is not mentioned.

5   E is correct. Mia mentions that she 'forgot about the last year' and advises Josh to 'stay in touch so they (the university) know your module choices'. The words 'making arrangements' are misleading word spots for 'make' and 'arrangements' in A.

NARRATOR: 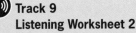 **Track 10**
Listening Worksheet 2

JOSH: Hi Mia, I wanted to ask you about the year abroad option. Would you recommend doing that?

MIA: Yes, definitely. It's a fantastic chance to study in another country for a year.

JOSH: I think I'd like to do it, but it looks very competitive – there's only a limited number of places.

MIA: Yes, so next year when you are in the **second year** of the course, you need to work really hard in all your theatre studies modules. <u>Only students with good marks get places – you have to prove that you know your subject really well.</u>

JOSH: Right. So how did you **choose where to go**?

MIA: Well, I decided <u>I wanted a programme that would fit in with what I wanted to do after I graduate, so I looked for a programme with emphasis on acting rather than directing for example.</u> It depends on you.

JOSH: OK. Was it easy to get what you wanted?

MIA: Well, about six months before you go, you have to **send in your choices**. <u>I had a friend who missed the deadline and didn't get her first choice, so you do need to get a move on at that stage.</u> You'll find that certain places are very popular with everyone.

JOSH: And don't you have to **write a personal statement** at that stage?

MIA: Yes.

JOSH: Right. <u>I'll get some of the final-year students to give me some tips</u> … maybe see if I can read what they wrote when they applied.

MIA: I think that's a very good idea. I don't mind showing you what I did. And while you're **doing your year abroad**, don't make the mistake I made. <u>I got so involved I forgot all about making arrangements for when I came back here for the last year. Make sure you stay in touch so they know your choices for the optional modules.</u> You don't want to miss out doing your preferred specialisms.

JOSH: Right. That's really helpful …

Get it right!

See underlining in Track 11.

1 actually   2 more useful   3 better off   4 it's best

NARRATOR: **Track 11**
Listening Worksheet 2

NARRATOR: 1
SPEAKER: Well, <u>actually</u> you need to go reception about that.

NARRATOR: 2
SPEAKER: Telephoning the business centre would be <u>more useful</u>.

NARRATOR: 3
SPEAKER: You'd be <u>better off</u> organising it yourself.

NARRATOR: 4
SPEAKER: Hm I understand, but <u>it's best</u> if you wait for them to contact you.

8

See underlining in Track 12.

1 the tutor / tutor
2 'online' / 'checking online' The answer 'business centre' is incorrect. The question asks 'how'.
3 the administrator
4 'wait' The answer 'wait for them' is incorrect because the question says no more than TWO WORDS and 'wait for them' is THREE WORDS.

NARRATOR: **Track 12**
Listening Worksheet 2

NARRATOR: 1
WOMAN: I'm sure the supervisor will help me with my assignment.

MAN: Well, actually you need to go to the office and speak to the <u>tutor</u> about that. Our supervisor may not give you the correct advice.

NARRATOR: 2
WOMAN: I thought I'd go to the library and find out more information.

MAN: Hm … you could, the library has one or two books about the topic, but <u>checking online</u> at the business centre would be a better idea.

NARRATOR: 3
WOMAN: I'm going to ask my mentor about my accommodation later today.

MAN: Well, I went to my mentor for help, but you'd be better off going to the office and talking to the <u>administrator</u>.

NARRATOR: 4
WOMAN: I sent the application last week. I'll chase them when I get home.

MAN: No, it's best if you <u>wait</u> for them to contact you.

---

9 Test task

See underlining in Track 13 for the position of the answers and bold text for signposting.

1   B is correct. Although Alex suggests he can 'find out about a particular company' which connects to F, Eva says, 'You'd be better off', which shows she is going to contradict Alex's idea. Eva then mentions 'using them to talk though what's available', which is a paraphrase for 'discuss options' in the option.

2   F is correct. Eva says, 'make contact with employers and find out more about them', which is a paraphrase for 'obtain company information' in the option.

3   G is correct. Eva says, 'chance of being interviewed' which connects to E; however, she goes on to talk about STEP, suggesting that Alex should go online and 'sign up with them'.

4   A is correct. Alex says, 'keep me informed about the progress of my application', which is a paraphrase for 'get updates' in the option. You may have connected the word 'informed' in the text to the word 'informing' in D; however, this is a misleading word spot. Eva says the mentor works 'with STEP', which connects to G; however, there is no mention of registering.

5   E is correct. Alex tentatively suggests going to the human resources department to 'find out what's going on', which connects with A; however, Eva rejects this by saying 'Not really'. She goes on to say that they will notify Alex if they want him to go for an interview and he will need to 'reply directly and confirm that you can attend'.

6   C is correct. Eva says that Alex will need to contact the tutor if he's been 'offered a job' which connects with D; however, this is because the tutor needs to 'provide a reference'. Eva mentions 'STEP' and 'company' but these are word spots for G and F.

NARRATOR: **Track 13**
Listening Worksheet 2

ALEX: Hi Eva, could you spare a few minutes to talk about the work placement you did last summer?

EVA: Sure. It was a fantastic experience.

ALEX: Yeah, I want to apply for a placement. How do I go about doing it?

EVA:	Well, first I'd go and visit the **careers officer**.
ALEX:	Right, I guess they can help me find out about a particular company?
EVA:	You'd be better off <u>using them to talk though what's available</u>. They've got all the relevant knowledge about the jobs market.
ALEX:	Right, OK.
EVA:	And you could also attend a **work experience fair**. There's one coming up at the end of the month.
ALEX:	Yes, I read about that.
EVA:	Great. Well, they're free for students and you can <u>make contact with employers and find out more about them.</u>
ALEX:	OK. I'll try and go.
EVA:	And then when you know what you want, you need to **go online**.
ALEX:	What's that for?
EVA:	Well, so that you have the best chance of being interviewed, there's an organisation, STEP. <u>You should sign up with them</u>. It's a fairly straightforward process.
ALEX:	Once I've done that, I understand that I'll be assigned a **mentor**. Is that right?
EVA:	Yes, that's right; they work with STEP.
ALEX:	And they will <u>keep me informed about the progress of my application</u>?
EVA:	Spot on.
ALEX:	I don't suppose it's a good idea to get in touch with the **human resource department** directly, is it? You now, to find out what's going on?
EVA:	Not really … but it is them who <u>will notify you if they want you to go for an interview. You'll get an email and, of course, you need to reply directly and confirm you can attend</u>.
ALEX:	Right … So, once I've had an interview, I should let **my tutor** know what the outcome is?
EVA:	Yes, you need to let her know if you've been offered a job so she can <u>provide you with a reference</u>. She knows your academic ability; your qualities, etcetera better than STEP will, and the company are definitely going to ask for one.
ALEX:	Well, thanks very much for the information – I'm starting to look forward …

Listening Worksheet 3

1

1   B is correct. Zack says, 'mainstream films have great special effects'; however, Ellie corrects him by saying, 'they might, but not necessarily'.

2   A is correct. Zack talks about independent films needing prize money and says that he will 'go with that' (choose that answer). Ellie confirms this by saying, 'Correct!'

3   B is correct. Zack mentions 'private investors'; however, this is in the context of independent films and is a word spot for A.

4   A is correct. Ellie mentions 'nine', but goes on to self-correct by saying, 'I … realised just in time that I was about to make a mistake. There are two fewer than I thought', which means there are seven.

NARRATOR:	🔊 **Track 14** **Listening Worksheet 3**
ZACK:	Hey, what are you doing Ellie?
ELLIE:	Oh hi Zack, I've just done this short quiz about films and filmmaking online. I got ten out of ten.
ZACK:	Cool. Let's have a go.
ELLIE:	Sure, right. Let's see, question one, what is a mainstream film? Is it a film with lots of special effects or one produced by a large production company?
ZACK:	Hm, I know this one. Right. Mainstream films have great special effects – I mean like 3D, animation and stuff.
ELLIE:	Well, they might, but not necessarily.
ZACK:	Oh right, so B's the correct answer then.
ELLIE:	That's right.
ZACK:	OK, number two.
ELLIE:	So, this is about film festival competitions. Like, best script or best screenplay. Who enters these, independent or studio films?
ZACK:	Well, I know that independent films need prize money to fund their film productions, so I'm going to go with that.
ELLIE:	Correct! Number three. How are studio films funded?
ZACK:	Well, on the basis that independent films either fund themselves or try and get money from other sources, like private investors, I'd say the studio does it. You know like, Warner Bros or Universal Pictures.

ELLIE:	Correct again! Well done. Next question. How many stages are there in the filmmaking process?
ZACK:	Goodness, how do you expect me to know that?
ELLIE:	It's hard. I thought nine initially but realised just in time that I was about to make a mistake. There are two fewer than I thought.
ZACK:	Hm well, you should know it, you are doing that film studies course. Right next …

2

1   video animation
2   seven / 7 (stages)
3   No. Stage 6 does not have a gap.
4   A singular noun is needed. You know this as the article 'a' comes before the gap.

3

See underlining in Track 15.

1   client

NARRATOR: 🔊 **Track 15**
Listening Worksheet 3

RIA:	Hi Stan, have you got a minute to talk our work placement? Specifically, the film and video animation project we are working on?
STAN:	Ah animation: the method of creating movement by showing a series of pictures one after the other very quickly.
RIA:	Argggh stop! You sound like our tutor.
STAN:	Ha. Sorry. OK. I'm not too sure about all the stages actually. Let me get a pen so I can write them down. Right: The video animation process.
RIA:	Ready? Good. Well, <u>the first thing is</u> to have a meeting to find out exactly what is required.
STAN:	Right. So we have to get together with the <u>client</u> and get a detailed understanding of the project.

4

See underlining in Track 15.

C 'The first thing is …' tells the listener the speaker is about to talk about their first point.

5

See underlining in Track 16.

2 structure   3 voice   4 drawings   5 colour   6 music

NARRATOR: 🔊 **Track 16**
Listening Worksheet 3

RIA:	Hi Stan, have you got a minute to talk about our work placement? Specifically, the film and video animation project we are working on?
STAN:	Ah animation: the method of creating movement by showing a series of pictures one after the other very quickly.
RIA:	Argggh stop! You sound like our tutor.
STAN:	Ha. Sorry. OK. I'm not too sure about all the stages actually. First, let me get a pen so I can write them down. Right: The video animation process.
RIA:	Ready? Good. Well, the first thing is to have a meeting to find out exactly what is required.
STAN:	Right. So, we have to get together with the <u>client</u> and get a detailed understanding of the project.
RIA:	Yes. That's right. Next, we **move** on to the idea or concept stage.
STAN:	Right. What happens then?
RIA:	Well, we have to put together a <u>structure</u> for the video that we are going to produce. Then, **once** that's been agreed, we start writing the script.
STAN:	That's really important.
RIA:	Absolutely.
STAN:	So, I've got that. We **then** have to find an actor using one of those online platforms.
RIA:	Right. One with the right sort of <u>voice</u> for our part.
STAN:	Yes. Their appearance doesn't matter as they won't be seen in the video. After **that**, a storyboard is put together. Can you remind me what that is?
RIA:	Well, just think of it as basic <u>drawings</u> which show the progress of the story scene by scene. We include a description of the visuals and the actions too.
STAN:	Great, that's clearer.
RIA:	Then we create the visual style, which means we add <u>colour</u> and things behind the character, like clouds, furniture or pets. This stage can take a long time.
STAN:	When can we get on to the exciting part and get the images moving?
RIA:	The **following** step, animation, is probably my favourite. Everything starts to come to life.

6

See bold text in Track 16.

1 move   2 once   3 then   4 that
5 following   6 finish

7

See underlining in Track 17.

1 illustrate   2 final   3 words   4 looked
5 begin   6 talked

NARRATOR: 🔊 **Track 17**
Listening Worksheet 3

RIA: To <u>illustrate</u> this point, let me tell you about what I did at the film studio.

STAN: This brings me to my <u>final</u> point, which is the development of special effects.

RIA: So, in other <u>words</u>, the reason I chose film studies was because …

STAN: OK, so we've <u>looked</u> at the challenges of scriptwriting …

RIA: I'd like to <u>begin</u> by describing the film production process.

STAN: I've <u>talked</u> about the role of the director …

8

A 2 and 5   B 1   C 3   D 4 and 6

9   Test task

See underlining in Track 18.

1   'script' is correct. The speaker says, 'an idea is turned into', which is a paraphrase for 'development of' in the question. Although the speaker mentions nouns, such as 'films', these are all plural nouns and the article 'a' before the gap tells you the answer must be a singular noun.

2   'planning' is correct. The speaker says, 'narrowed down' which is a paraphrase for 'reduced' in the question.

3   'managers' is correct. The words 'are employed' in the question indicate you are listening for a job title in the plural form. The speaker mentions 'producer'; however, this is a singular form. Also, the speaker goes on to say the producer is 'already in place' which means already employed.

4   'budget' is correct. The speakers say, 'It's really important that the company sticks to agreed activities' which is a paraphrase for a 'schedule must be followed' in the question.

5   'Communication' is correct. As with Question 4, this question is in the **production** stage of the process. The speaker uses the phrase, 'In addition' to tell you that the answer is coming. The word 'crucial' in the text is a paraphrase for 'very important' in the question.

6   'wages' is correct. The speaker says, 'Now let's turn to' to signal that they are changing topic and moving to the next stage: photography. The words, 'things get particularly costly at this point' are a paraphrase for 'An expensive stage' in the question.

7   'remote' is correct. The speaker says, 'filming might be in locations' which is a paraphrase for 'filming in … places'.

8   'suppliers' is correct. The speaker says, 'Once that's done' to signpost that they are moving to the next stage. The speaker mentions 'the company'; however, 'the company' is incorrect because it is two words and 'to company' is not grammatically correct.

9   'studio' is correct. Before the gap, the words 'in the' suggest that you are listening for a place.

10   'cinemas' is correct. Although there is not direct paraphrase for 'are sent to' in the question, 'over the internet', is a paraphrase for 'online platforms'. The word 'films' fits grammatically; however, it cannot be the correct answer because 'Films are sent to films' does not make sense.

NARRATOR: 🔊 **Track 18**
Listening Worksheet 3

LECTURER: Hello everyone and welcome to this afternoon's short presentation about film production. Before we start, I just want to remind you that after the presentation, the university film club will be showing photographic images from their project, 'Films Through The Ages', so please do stay for that if you can. OK right, so coming back to this afternoon's topic, film production, you can see from the slide that there are seven stages.

Now, although production projects are not all the same, they typically start with development. Not all ideas for films start out as original concepts – they may, for instance, come from books, other films or true stories. But in each case, an idea is turned into a <u>script</u> and after approval, writers come up with an initial outline of the film.

Moving on, we come to pre-production. At the start of this stage, the company has a number of different production

---

options. Once these have been narrowed down, planning begins; the vision of the project is decided, and then the producer, who is already in place, is in a position to hire managers and decide where they are going to film.

This brings us to production. During this stage, decisions are made about how the company intends to film day to day.

It's really important that the company sticks to agreed activities so that it doesn't exceed its budget – everything has to be well-controlled. In addition, if the process is to run smoothly, it's crucial that there's communication with everyone involved in the process.

Now let's turn to photography – when the camera finally starts to roll. As you can imagine, things get particularly costly at this point. There are wages to consider, filming might be in locations which are remote and difficult to get to, and there are special effects which are becoming more and more technical.

Once that's done, we've got the period immediately after filming, which is called the 'wrap'. This is when the set gets taken down and put away, the site is cleared and suppliers get back anything the company borrowed or hired.

After this we have postproduction. The film is taken back, typically to the studio, to where it is viewed and edited before the final stage of the process, which is what I want to talk briefly about now.

This is distribution. Of course, the film must be distributed for the producers to make a profit, or at least to get back their original investment. Of course, by the time we come to view films in cinemas or quite possibly these days, over the internet, we might forget all the hard work that went into making them. Right, that's the seven stages in the process I wanted to highlight today; you'll find more details in the reading I gave you …

Listening Worksheet 4

1

1   B A fork in the road (or river) is when it divides into two parts.

2   C You might hear 'round the bend' or 'round the corner'.

3   A You might hear 'junction', 'crossroads' or 'intersection'.

2a

1 Map C

NARRATOR: 🔊 Track 19
Listening Worksheet 4

MAN: Excuse me. Where is Maybrook School?

WOMAN: OK, so this is Main Street …

MAN: Yes, I've just come from the bus station round the corner on Hallam Road.

WOMAN: OK, well, go along Main Street, past the museum, until you come to a hotel on the corner. Take a right at the lights – that's Mill Street. You can't miss the school – it's just past the park opposite the carpark.

2b

1   go along
2   Take a right
3   just past

Get it right!

1 up   2 through   3 round   4 over   5 rear
6 centre   7 before   8 alongside

NARRATOR: 🔊 Track 20
Listening Worksheet 4

MAN: OK, so you need to walk up this road until you reach the lights.

WOMAN: Once in the main hall you need to go through the door on the right.

MAN: Just round the bend you will find the coffee shop.

WOMAN: Go over the bridge and into the forest.

MAN: You have to enter via the rear of the building.

WOMAN: You'll find the fountain in the centre of the park.

MAN: Just before you reach the lake, there is the picnic area.

WOMAN: The river runs alongside the railway line so you can see it from the train.

3

See underlining in Track 21.

1 D is correct. The correct option is G: opposite the school, just to the right of the beautiful park.
2 C is correct: it is halfway down Main Street directly opposite the surgery.
3 A is incorrect. A is at the end of Mill Street; however, it is next to the bus station. E is the correct answer: just behind the museum at the far end of Mill Street.

NARRATOR: 🔊 **Track 21**
Listening Worksheet 4

MAN: Here's the map of the town centre. It's not to scale, of course, but anyway on the map, you can see the school on Main Street and the bank is <u>opposite the school, just to the right of the beautiful park.</u> There's a great play area there for kids. OK if you need refreshments, there's a coffee shop located <u>halfway down Main Street directly opposite the surgery</u>. It's open seven days a week and the homemade cakes are great. Finally, then, there's the new science centre <u>just behind the museum at the far end of Mill Street.</u> OK that's all I wanted to say for now …

4

See underlining in Track 22.

1 just to the right of   2 on the corner   3 halfway down

NARRATOR: 🔊 **Track 22**
Listening Worksheet 4

MAN: Firstly, we'll plant mature pine trees to provide shelter and shade <u>just to the right of</u> the supermarket …

To address the traffic problems, the pavements <u>on the corner of</u> Carberry Street and Thomas Street will be widened …

Something we're planning to do to help control the flow of traffic in the area is to install traffic lights <u>halfway down</u> Hill Street …

5

See underlining in Track 23.

1 C '<u>just to the right of the supermarket in Days Road</u>'
2 D 'the pavements <u>on the corner of Carberry and Thomas Street</u>'
3 G 'the roadway <u>at the entry of Thomas Street from Days Road</u> will be painted red'
4 B 'A "keep clear" sign will be erected <u>at the junction of Evelyn Street and Hill Street</u>.'
5 F 'install traffic lights <u>halfway down Hill Street where it crosses Days Road</u>'

6 A '<u>on the other side of Hill Street from the supermarket</u>'
7 E '<u>at the other end of Hill Street close to the intersection with Carberry Street</u>'

NARRATOR: 🔊 **Track 23**
Listening Worksheet 4

MAN: Now, we've also put together a map which we've sent out to all the residents in the area. And on the map, we've marked the proposed changes. Firstly, we'll plant mature pine trees to provide shelter and shade <u>just to the right of the supermarket in Days Road</u>.

To address the traffic problems, the pavements <u>on the corner of Carberry and Thomas Street will be widened</u>. This will help to reduce the speed of vehicles entering Thomas Street.

We think it's very important to separate the local residential streets from the main road. So, the roadway <u>at the entry of Thomas Street from Days Road</u> will be painted red. This should mark it more clearly and act as a signal for traffic to slow down.

One way of making sure that the pedestrians are safe is to increase signage at the intersection. <u>A 'keep clear' sign will be erected at the junction of Evelyn Street and Hill Street</u>, to enable traffic to exit at all times.

Something we're planning to do to help control the flow of traffic in the area is to install traffic lights <u>halfway down Hill Street where it crosses Days Road</u>.

Now we haven't thought about only the cars and traffic, of course; there's also something for the children. We're going to get school children in the area to research a local story, the life of a local sports hero perhaps, and an artist will incorporate that story into paintings on the wall of a building <u>on the other side of Hill Street from the supermarket.</u>

And finally, we've agreed to build a new children's playground which will be <u>at the other end of Hill Street close to the intersection</u> with Carberry Street.

6

1 in the southeast   2 in the far northwest
3 to the east   4 south of
5 just on the west   6 near the north

7 Test task

See underlining in Track 24.

1 A 'there's a lake in the northwest of the park, with a bird hide to the west of it, at the end of a path'

2 I 'close to where refreshments are available … in the southern part of the park, leading off from the path'.

3 F 'the circular area on the map surrounded by paths'

4 E 'in the western section of the park, between two paths'

5 D 'along the path which takes you to the east gate'

NARRATOR: **Track 24**
Listening Worksheet 4

PARK CO-ORDINATOR: Hello everyone. I'd like to tell you about our new wildlife area, Hinchingbrooke Park, which will be opened to the public next month. This slide doesn't really indicate how big it is, but anyway, you can see the two gates into the park, and the main paths.

As you can see, there's a lake in the northwest of the park, with a bird hide to the west of it, at the end of a path. So it'll be a nice quiet place for watching the birds on the water.

Fairly close to where refreshments are available, there's a dog-walking area in the southern part of the park, leading off from the path.

And if you just want to sit and relax, you can go to the flower garden; that's the circular area on the map surrounded by paths.

For those who want some shade, there's a wooded area in the western section of the park, between two paths.

If you need to use the facilities, the toilet block is located just along the path which takes you to the east gate. It's right on the path so you can't miss it. OK, that's enough from me, so let's go on to …

Listening Worksheet 5

1

See underlining in Track 25.

They've all inspired modern technology.

NARRATOR: **Track 25**
Listening Worksheet 5

ANNA: Hi Kennie, what are you up to?

KENNIE: Hi Anna, I'm just reading an article online. Here, look at these photos and tell me what the connection is.

ANNA: Erm, Well, they're not people? They're all found in the wild?

KENNIE: Nope. You'll never guess.

ANNA: Go on then … tell me.

KENNIE: They've all, in different ways, inspired advances in modern technology.

ANNA: Really? Wow, tell me more …

Get it right!

a and b

1, 2, 3 and 4 are incorrect because the candidate made simple mistakes.

A 1 and 2 For Question 1, 'River walk' might be the correct answer; however, the instructions say NO MORE THAN TWO WORDS and the candidate has written THREE words. For Question 2, the answer might be 'small' as it fits grammatically; however, the candidate included a number (£10) which was not included in the instructions. If you need to listen for numbers, the instructions will include AND/OR A NUMBER.

B 4 The base word 'camera' might be correct; however, it does not fit grammatically – we know this because the plural verb 'are' just before the gap tells us a plural noun is needed. The candidate probably heard the word 'cameras' but wrote 'camera' in error.

C 3 The heading of this column is 'Event', so the answer 'Wednesday', which is a day not an event, is incorrect. The candidate probably didn't use the headings to help them predict the answers and follow the speaker as they were listening.

2

1 ~~book~~ 2 ~~concern~~ 3 ~~boys~~ 4 ~~girl~~ 5 ~~museum~~
6 ~~days~~ 7 ~~dog~~ 8 ~~animal~~ 9 ~~idea~~ 10 ~~things~~

3

3 What could be on a gecko's feet? (plural noun) What part of a gecko's foot might be sticky?

4 What things do climbers use? (plural noun) What things have been made for climbers? Shoes? Ropes?

5 Where do kingfishers go? What do kingfishers do? (verb). What do kingfishers need their beaks for? Eat?

6 Where do the trains go?

4

See underlining in Track 26.

1 'skin'

2 'boats' Kennie mentions 'spaceships' but then uses the word 'actually' to signpost that he is going to correct that idea.

3 'hairs' Kennie uses the phrase 'thousands of' which tells you it must be a plural noun and not a singular one.

4 'gloves' The words 'developed special' without an article, 'a' or 'the', indicate that you are listening for a plural or uncountable noun. In the table, a singular noun will not fit grammatically ('have been made', not 'has been made').

5 'dive' The verb 'catch' is mentioned; however, this is in connection with 'food' and not with doing something 'silently' (so it can catch food).

6 'tunnels' The words 'when the trains went through' without an article, 'a' or 'the', indicate you need a plural or uncountable noun.

NARRATOR: **Track 26**
Listening Worksheet 5

ANNA: Hi Kennie, what are you up to?

KENNIE: Hi Anna, I'm just reading an article online. Here, look at photos and tell me what the connection is?

ANNA: Erm, Well, they're totally different. Hm … they're not people? They're all found in the wild?

KENNIE: Nope. You'll never guess.

ANNA: Go on then … tell me.

KENNIE: They've all inspired modern technology.

ANNA: Really? Wow, tell me more.

KENNIE: OK, so let's start with this one.

ANNA: A shark! So why are scientists interested in them? Is it their teeth?

KENNIE: No. It's because they've got a pattern – not exactly scales, but a bit like that, all over their <u>skin. This helps them to move easily</u> and smoothly through the water because nothing can attach to it. Anyway, scientists from NASA became aware of this and decided to copy it. You'd think it'd be for spaceships – you know for coming through the atmosphere – but <u>actually it's for boats</u> to help them move faster.

ANNA: That makes sense, I guess.

KENNIE: Then there's geckos …

ANNA: Well, I know that they have light-sensitive eyes.

KENNIE: Yes, they're able to make various sounds to communicate, too. Anyway, they've got <u>thousands of hairs on the bottom of their feet</u> so they can climb without falling. They can even walk on smooth ceilings or climb up glass walls. And as well as that, scientists have already <u>developed special gloves for rock climbers</u> based on the same principle and they hope one day to be able to catch rubbish in space.

ANNA: That would be cool. What about the kingfisher – such a beautiful bird.

KENNIE: It is. Right, well a kingfisher's habitat is slow-flowing rivers and lakes. Because they have an aerodynamic beak – pointed and shaped like a spear – when they <u>dive</u> into water to catch food, <u>it's noiseless</u>. A bird-loving Japanese engineer redesigned the high-speed bullet trains using the same idea. The problem they were having with <u>loud booms when the trains went through tunnels disappeared</u>.

ANNA: Goodness. How interesting. Let's find out what other animals have inspired …

---

5 Test task

See underlining in Track 27.

1 'Frogs' The speaker says, 'The first species to generate a lot of interesting information was frogs.' The omission of an article ('a' or 'the') indicates a plural form is needed.

2 'owls' The speaker mentions the phrase 'urban areas', which is a paraphrase for 'in cities' in the table.

3 'count' The phrase 'no difficulties with our efforts to precisely' is a paraphrase for 'Easy to … accurately' in the table.

4 'seeds' The phrase 'a variety of' in the table indicates you need a plural noun. The plural noun 'plants' is mentioned by the speaker; however, the plants produce the seeds which the birds eat: 'buying lots of different plants meaning there's an extensive range of seeds around, which is what they feed on'.

5 'survey' The speaker uses the word 'massive', which is a synonym for 'large' in the table and 'about to be launched' means 'starting soon'.

---

6   'chemicals' The speaker says, 'Populations have recovered', which tells you the answer is coming (if you are using the headings to help you). The speaker's phrase 'decline from …' indicates something has been reduced (less use of).

7   'online' The speaker does not use a synonym for the word 'watch' in the table; however, they say, 'A webcam, originally installed for security purposes, now streams the pair's activities online' which implies that people watch the birds and that they do this online.

NARRATOR: **Track 27 Listening Worksheet 5**

TEACHER: Good morning. Today I'd like to present the findings of our Year 2 project on wildlife found in gardens throughout our city. The first species to generate a lot of interesting information was <u>frogs</u>. And there was a clear pattern here – they breed where there is water that's suitable. Garden ponds are on the rise, and rural ponds are disappearing, leading to massive migration to the towns. Hedgehogs are also finding it easier to live in urban areas – this time because <u>owls</u>, for example, that hunt hedgehogs at night, prefer not to leave the protection of their rural environment. We had lots of sightings, so all in all, we had no difficulties with our efforts to precisely <u>count</u> their numbers.

Our next species is the finest of bird singers, the song thrush. On the decline in the countryside, they are experiencing a revival in urban gardens because these days gardeners, like myself actually, are buying lots of different plants meaning there's an extensive range of <u>seeds</u> around, which is what they feed on.

Another factor is the provision of nesting places – which is actually better in gardens than the countryside. Hard to believe it, but it's true. Incidentally, we discovered that a massive new <u>survey</u> on their numbers is about to be launched, so you should keep an eye open for that.

Next, I'd like to talk about the peregrine falcon – the fastest bird in the world that can reach astonishing speeds of three hundred and twenty kilometres an hour. Populations have recovered following decades of decline from harmful <u>chemicals</u> used in farming and they now nest in over two hundred artificial or urban locations in the country. Nottingham Trent University's Newton building is home to one of the most famous pairs of peregrine falcons.

A webcam, originally installed for security purposes, now streams the pair's activities <u>online</u>. Right well, that's all I wanted to talk about this evening; however, please do stay for our spectacular photographic display when I'll be around to answer any questions you may have.

Listening Worksheet 6

1
See underlining in Track 28.
1 help   2 information   3 details   4 order   5 time
6 blank   7 Change

NARRATOR: **Track 28 Listening Worksheet 6**

JODIE: Hey, how's it going?

FRANK: Alright thanks. I'm just revising for my IELTS test.

JODIE: Me too! I'm worried about note completion questions. Can you give me some advice?

FRANK: Of course. Let me think. OK, first I'd suggest you **read the title and subtitles**. This will <u>help</u> you to follow what the speaker is saying.

JODIE: Got it.

FRANK: Then, it's important that you **consider**, for each question, the <u>information</u> that fits. So, if it could be a number, person, location or something else.

JODIE: OK. Understood. What else?

FRANK: Well, this part of the test is about testing your ability to listen for <u>details</u> not the general idea.

JODIE: That's hard.

FRANK: Yes, it is, but **don't forget that the questions** follow the same <u>order</u> as the listening text, so that makes it a bit easier.

JODIE: Right and what shouldn't I do?

FRANK: Well, you have thirty seconds or so to look at the questions **during the test**. Some people just look out the window, but that's really not a useful way to spend the <u>time</u> you have! Instead, you should study the questions and think about what the speaker might say.

JODIE: That's a good point.

FRANK: It is. Hm … right, next I'd say, **if you don't know** an answer, think about the meaning of the passage as a whole and write down something that might be possible. You might still get a mark. Obviously, you get no marks if a question is left <u>blank</u>.

JODIE: OK – I hadn't thought of that. Anything else?

FRANK: Hmm … yes *one more thing* and this is really important. Candidates sometimes <u>change</u> the verb tense or make a plural a singular and that's a *big mistake*. You must write exactly what you hear.

JODIE: Really, so if the speakers says, for example, 'house' and I write 'houses', or 'frogs' and I write 'frog', then it is wrong?

FRANK: Yep – that would usually be a wrong answer!

JODIE: Cool. That's really useful advice thanks …

2

See bold text in Track 28.

1 read the title and subtitles
2 consider
4 don't forget that the questions
5 during the test
6 if you don't know

3

See italic text in Track 28.

1 B The speaker says 'one more thing' to tell the listener that they are moving to their final point after all the other things they've said.

4 Possible paraphrases:

2 electronically
3 thinking of / inventing / having an idea / a plan for an object / a gadget
4 differently / in a different way
5 the same / not different   boring / dull

5

Sentence 2 – something belonging to Jonas connected to a competition

Sentence 3 – place / room

Sentence 4 – object connected to Jonas' design

Sentence 5 – some existing objects (maybe the things Jonas is focusing on / redesigning)

6a

See underlining in Track 29.

'tutor' We predicted the type of word needed for the first gap was a person. While two people are mentioned by Jonas, 'professor' and 'tutor', the phrase 'give me some support' is what the tutor said to Jonas, *not* what the professor said.

6b

See underlining in Track 29.   2 drawings
3 kitchen   4 technology   5 dishwashers

NARRATOR: 🔊 **Track 29**
Listening Worksheet 6

JONAS: Erm … hello Professor. I'm working on my entry for the Global Design Competition. My <u>tutor</u> said you might be able to give me some support.

PROFESSOR: Ah, yes, I got an electronic copy of your <u>drawings</u>. Come in and tell me about it. What sort of competition is it?

JONAS: Well, it's an international design competition and we have to come up with a new idea for a typical domestic <u>kitchen</u> appliance.

PROFESSOR: I see, and are there any special conditions? Does it have to save energy for example?

JONAS: Actually, that was the focus last year. This year's different. We have to develop an innovative idea for existing <u>technology</u>, using it in a way that hasn't been thought of before.

PROFESSOR: I see, that sounds tricky. And what have you chosen?

JONAS: Well, I decided to choose <u>dishwashers</u> because they are an everyday item in most Australian houses, but they're all pretty boring and almost identical to each other.

I think some people will be prepared to pay a little extra for something that looks different.

PROFESSOR: That's a nice idea …

7 Test task

See underlining in Track 30.

1 'starting' You know the answer is coming when you hear the professor and Jonas say the word 'stone'. 'The dishwasher' in the listening text is a paraphrase for 'the machine' in the question.

2 'clean' You know the answer is coming when Jonas says 'carbon dioxide'. The 'plates and cups' is a paraphrase for 'the dishes' in the question.

3 'waste' You know the answer is coming when you hear 'once the washing cycle is complete' in the listening text which is a paraphrase for 'At the end of the washing cycle' in the question.

4 'potential' 'reduce household costs' in the question is a paraphrase for 'save … money on their electricity bills' in the listening text. The listening text mentions the design is also 'good for the planet', but this what Jonas's tutor thinks (not what Jonas thinks).

5 'presentation' Jonas says, 'I was hoping you could help me with', which is a paraphrase for 'needs help' preparing for' in the question.

6 'model' Jonas's professor says, 'if you want to stand a good chance of winning you really need a …', which is a way of giving advice.

7 'materials' Jonas's professor asks, 'What is the main difficulty so far?', which tells you the answer is coming. The professor then suggests 'materials'. We know Jonas agrees because he says, 'Yes. I want it to look professional, but everything that's top quality is also very expensive.'

8 'grant' The professor says, 'why don't you talk to the university about', which is a way of making a suggestion.

9 'details' The professor asks Jonas to give him the report which implies that the professor is going to 'check' it. The word 'technical' is incorrect because it is an adjective and a noun ('the___') is needed in the gap.

NARRATOR: **Track 30**
Listening Worksheet 6

PROFESSOR: I see you've called your design 'the Rockpool'; why is that?

JONAS: Basically, because it looks like the rockpools you find on a beach. The top is made of glass so that you can look down into it.

PROFESSOR: And there's a stone at the bottom. Is that just for decoration?

JONAS: Actually, it does have a function. Instead of pushing a button, you turn the stone.

PROFESSOR: So it's really just a novel way of <u>starting the dishwasher</u>.

JONAS: That's right.

PROFESSOR: It's a really nice design, but what makes it innovative?

JONAS: Well, I decided to make a dishwasher that uses carbon dioxide.

PROFESSOR: In place of water and soap? How will you manage that?

JONAS: The idea is to pressurise it so that it becomes a liquid. The fluid is then released into the dishwasher so it can <u>clean the plates and cups</u>, etcetera, all by itself.

PROFESSOR: Sounds like a brilliant idea! Your system will totally stop the need for strong detergents, like soap. So, what happens once the washing cycle is complete?

JONAS: Well, to allow the contents to dry, the <u>waste all goes to an area called the holding chamber</u>. That's where the liquid is depressurised and changes back to a gas. Then the oil and grease are separated out and removed.

PROFESSOR: It sounds like you've thought it all out very thoroughly. So, do you think it'll ever be built?

JONAS: I don't see why not. It's energy efficient and has the <u>potential to save people quite a bit of money</u> on their electricity bills. My tutor pointed out that as it uses no harmful chemicals, it's good for the planet too.

PROFESSOR: Well, I'm sure a lot of positive things will come out of your design.

PROFESSOR: Now, you seem to have thought about everything so what exactly did you need me to help you with?

JONAS: Well, it's my final design submission, I've made it to the final stage of the competition, and, in a few months' time, I have to <u>give a presentation, and that's the part I was hoping you could help me with</u>.

PROFESSOR: Right, well that should be easy enough. What have you managed to do so far?

JONAS: Well, I've got detailed drawings to show how it will work and I've also written a five-hundred-word paper on it.

PROFESSOR:	I see. Well, if you want to stand a good chance of winning, <u>you really need a model of the machine</u>.
JONAS:	Yes, I thought I might but I'm having a few problems.
PROFESSOR:	What is the main difficulty so far? Let me guess – is it the <u>materials</u>?
JONAS:	Yes. I want it to look professional, but everything that's <u>top quality is also very expensive</u>.
PROFESSOR:	Look, projects like this are very important to us. They really help lift our profile. So why don't you talk to the university about a <u>grant</u>? I can help you <u>fill out the application forms</u> if you like.
JONAS:	That would be great.
PROFESSOR:	You'd better show me this paper you've written as well. For a global competition such as this, you need to <u>make sure the technical details you've given are accurate and thorough</u>.
JONAS:	That would be a great help.
PROFESSOR:	Is there anything else I can do?
JONAS:	Well, no I think that's it. Thanks, you've been really helpful …

Reading Worksheet 1

The underlining indicates where in the text the answers come from.

Reading task

1 B

We learn in Section A that it can be difficult to see the seahorses at first. The text says, 'When Goss brings friends to snorkel in the pool, <u>they can spend ages searching in vain for seahorses</u>. But as soon as he points one out and they know what to look for, they realise these creatures are everywhere.'

A is incorrect because the water the seahorses live in is not deep. The text says the pool of water is 'a mere 13m in depth'.

C is incorrect because the text describes the area as '<u>a bit of a hidden secret</u> and local people are keen to keep it that way, at least for now'. This means the area is not easily accessible.

D is incorrect because the text says, '<u>But most incredible of all, this little-surveyed ecosystem is home to the world's largest known population of seahorses</u>'. This means that they have not been studied widely.

2 D

The process of counting the seahorses takes a long time. The text talks about the different stages involved – catching the seahorses, injecting them and making repeat visits in order to complete the process. The text says, '<u>The procedure involves</u> carefully <u>catching</u> the creatures, <u>injecting</u> a dot of harmless coloured dye under their skin, then <u>letting them go</u> again. <u>Repeat visits</u> to the area will provide an estimate of how many animals come and go, and a rough idea of the total population size.'

A is incorrect because the method used to count the seahorses is safe and does not injure them. The text says they are injected with 'a dot of <u>harmless coloured dye</u> under their skin'.

B is incorrect because the text says that this same counting method is used with other animal species. The text refers to the method as '<u>a classic technique for estimating animal numbers</u> [that] often works well for seahorses'.

C is incorrect because the method does not produce precise information – it only provides a rough estimate of seahorse numbers. The text says, 'Because of their particularly active nature, <u>she experienced some trouble finding the marked seahorses again … she has yet to come up with a definitive number</u> of seahorses'.

3 B

We learn in Section C that these seahorses are different from other lined seahorses. They have unique, distinguishing features that set them apart. The text says, 'She began to wonder if the species were interbreeding, but <u>genetic studies</u> which involved sequencing two of the seahorses' genes, <u>showed that these are in fact lined seahorses, but unlike others of that species</u>.'

A is incorrect because we do not know for sure how the seahorses got into the pool. The text makes reference to <u>one theory</u> put forward that '<u>it could be the case that somebody put them there</u>. There is a long history of people in the Bahamas using natural pools for aquaculture, <u>perhaps stocking them with fish</u> to grow bigger and multiply', but this is not presented as a fact in the text.

C is incorrect because the text does not say that the seahorses arrived in the pool in large numbers. The text says, '<u>It may be that a few young seahorses</u> managed to swim through these holes in the rock separating the two bodies of water.'

D is incorrect because although the text mentions sea levels, it does not state as fact that the seahorses arrived in the pool because of a change in sea levels. The text merely speculates and suggests that '<u>one other theory is that</u> they were left behind by falling sea levels in the past'.

4 A

The text explains that the seahorses have adapted very successfully to their pool habitat – they have evolved shorter tails because the pool is easy to swim in and longer heads which the writer explains may be because of the food available to them in the pool and the way they need to feed. The text says, 'their tails are shorter and stubbier than normal. This is likely because their self-contained environment lacks the currents of the open ocean and so it is much easier to swim in … They also have longer, more slender heads than their open-seas cousins. This may have something to do with the way seahorses feed and the type of food available in the pool'.

B is incorrect because the text does not say that the diet of the seahorses has expanded. All we are told is that they 'eat tiny shrimps and plankton'. This means they have a limited diet.

C is incorrect because the text does not compare the physical conditions of the pool and the open sea in detail. All we are told is that the pool 'lacks the currents of the open ocean'.

D is incorrect because the text does not compare the feeding behaviour of the seahorses with other species. We are just told about the feeding behaviour of the seahorses in the pool and are given a description of the 'pipette feeding' process they use.

5 C

We learn in the text that 'In recent years, there have been incidences of people deliberately removing them from the pool and the risk of that continuing is high'.

A is incorrect – although there is a threat of chemical pollution in future, it is not affecting the seahorses in the pool at the moment. The text says there are 'real fears that chemical run-off from pesticides and fertilisers could contaminate the water quality'.

B is incorrect because harbour development has not happened yet, but may do so in the future. The text says, 'Another threat is the possibility that the pool could be turned into a marina – the Bahamas lacks protected harbours and there are plenty of people willing to pay good money for somewhere to moor up their boats.'

D is incorrect because the seahorses are not currently affected by farming methods. The text says, 'Agricultural practices in the area are also moving increasingly close to the pool's borders …'

6 B

The text tells us that the seahorses are 'secretive' in that they inhabit a very secluded, isolated pool and that their physical characteristics and habits are still not fully understood. The text also tells us that they have adapted to cope with their habitat – evolving shorter tails and longer heads. They have also developed a specific method of feeding. This means that they are

'facing the challenges of the changing world'. This changing world includes the threats described in Section E of the text – possible disturbance of their habitat by harbour development, etc.

A is incorrect because there is still a lot that researchers need to learn about the seahorses.

C is incorrect because seahorse numbers in the pool are healthy – there are thousands of them so they are not 'very close to extinction'.

D is incorrect because both researchers and local people are keen to protect the habitat of the seahorses and they are not forgotten. This is the focus of Section F.

1a and 1b

1 B (See Section A) 2 A (See Section C)
3 B (See Section C) 4 B (See Section D)
5 A (See Section D) 6 A (See Section E)

2

a system of assessment	Section B
the arrival of the seahorses into the pool	Section C
a little-known location	Section A
how the seahorses are developing	Section D

3a and 3b

Suggested answers:

Section E: Dangers faced by the seahorses

Section E: Efforts to protect seahorses and their habitat

4a, b, c and d

1 What do we learn about the seahorses in Eleuthera in the first section?
A They live in deep waters. *Not shallow*
B They can initially be difficult to spot. *Not easy to see at first*
C They inhabit an area that is easily accessible. *Live in a place that's easy to reach*
D They have been extensively studied. *A lot of research has been done on them*

2 According to the passage, the method used to count seahorses
A can cause injury to the animal. *Can harm or hurt them*
B is seldom used on other species. *Rarely done on other animals*
C produces precise information. *Provides very accurate data*
D takes a long time to complete. *Takes ages to finish*

Jonas (See answers to reading task for reasons.)

5a

Facts:

is technically known as

is a long history

All that we know for sure is

Speculation:

It may be that

it could be the case that

One other theory is that

5b

B (See answers to reading task for explanation.)

6

A   C

7a and b

Positive

Seahorse numbers are healthy.

They have adapted to life in the pool.

Local people and researchers want to protect them.

Students' own titles

7c

B (See answers to reading task for explanation.)

Exercise 8 test practice task

1 C

The text says, 'Early 20th-century biologists came to a similar conclusion, though they qualified it in terms of probability, stating there is no reason why evolution cannot run backwards – it is just very unlikely. And so the idea of irreversibility in evolution stuck and came to be known as "Dollo's law".'

A is incorrect because the text does not say that it was 'immediately referred to as Dollo's law'. The text says, 'And so the idea of irreversibility in evolution stuck and came to be known as "Dollo's law".'

B is incorrect because the text states the opposite. Dollo's theory rejected the possibility of evolutionary throwbacks. The text says, 'a Belgian palaeontologist called Louis Dollo was studying fossil records and coming to the opposite conclusion. In 1890 he proposed that evolution was irreversible: "that an organism is unable to return, even partially, to a previous stage already realised in the ranks of its ancestors".'

D is incorrect because the text does not state it was not based on many years of research.

2 D

The text says, 'exceptions have been cropping up. In 1919, for example, a humpback whale with a pair of leg-like appendages over a metre long, complete with a full set of limb bones, was caught off Vancouver Island in Canada. Explorer Roy Chapman Andrews argued at the time that the whale must be a throwback to a land-living ancestor. "I can see no other explanation", he wrote in 1921'.

A is incorrect because the text does not say that the whole body of the humpback whale was big – it emphasises the length of the limbs. The text says, 'with a pair of leg-like appendages over a metre long, complete with a full set of limb bones'.

B is incorrect because the humpback whale example does not support Dollo's law. Dollo's law rejects the possibility of evolutionary throwbacks. The text says, 'If Dollo's law is right, atavisms should occur only very rarely, if at all. Yet almost since the idea took root, exceptions have been cropping up'.

C is incorrect because the text does not make reference to a lot of controversy. The text only mentions one reaction by an explorer. The text says, 'Explorer Roy Chapman Andrews argued at the time that the whale must be a throwback to a land-living ancestor.'

3 C

The text says, 'If these silent genes are somehow switched back on, they argued, long-lost traits could reappear.'

A is incorrect because their numbers vary randomly and not according to species.

The text says, 'Silent genes accumulate random mutations, they reasoned, eventually rendering them useless.'

B is incorrect – there is no reference in the text to Raff disagreeing with the use of the term 'silent genes'.

D is incorrect because the text makes reference to possible lifespans. So, they do not have 'an unlimited lifespan'. The text says, 'The team calculated that there is a good chance of silent genes surviving for up to 6 million years in at least a few individuals in a population, and that some might survive for as long as 10 million years.'

4 B

The text says, 'The salamander example fits with Raff's 10-million-year time frame.'

A is incorrect because the mole salamander does not develop in the same way as 'most other amphibians.' The text says, 'The simplest explanation for this is that the axolotl lineage alone lost the ability to metamorphose, while others retained it. From a detailed analysis of the salamanders' family tree, however, it is clear that the other lineages evolved from an ancestor that itself had lost the ability to metamorphose.'

C is incorrect because the text does not refer to more than one ability. Only one ability is mentioned – the ability to metamorphose. The paragraph about mole salamanders focuses solely on this one ability.

D is incorrect because the text does not say that the ancestors of the mole salamander have been studied extensively. The text only makes reference to 'a detailed analysis of the salamanders' family tree'.

5 A

The text makes reference to the fact that members of the Bachia lizard family have lost toes and then re-evolved them. The text says, 'The simplest explanation is that the toed lineages never lost their toes, but <u>Wagner begs to differ. According to his analysis of the Bachia family tree, the toed species re-evolved toes from toeless</u> ancestors and, what is more, <u>digit loss and gain has occurred on more than one occasion over tens of millions of years</u>.'

B is incorrect because there is no reference to the environment as a causal factor in the evolution of the Bachia lizard.

C is incorrect because Wagner's research goes against Raff's assertion that there is a 10-million-year time frame. The text says, '<u>More recently, however, examples have been reported that break the time limit, suggesting that silent genes may not be the whole story</u>.' The text goes on to report on Wagner's findings that the evolution has occurred over '<u>tens of millions of years</u>'.

D is incorrect because the text does not make reference to any other species of South American lizards.

Reading Worksheet 2

1

1 bobsled   2 figure skating   3 luge
4 Nordic combined   5 biathlon   6 skeleton
7 puck   8 triple axel   9 slalom   10 double cork 1080

2

bobsled (paragraph 1); downhill skiing (paragraph 1); skeleton (paragraph 1); slalom (paragraph 4); skateboarding (paragraph 5); figure skating (paragraph 5); ice hockey (paragraph 8)

3

2   <u>Winter Olympic athletes</u> are born with <u>high sensation-seeking personalities</u>.
3   <u>The desire to try new things</u> is part of <u>human nature</u>.

4

Anya is correct.

5

1   NOT GIVEN The writer refers to the skeleton as 'terrifying' and goes on to mention the speed at which the athlete must travel and the fact that the sport involves going 'head first' implying that it is risky. However, the text does not say that it 'carries a higher level of risk' compared with the other Olympic sports mentioned.

2   NOT GIVEN The text talks about 'elite athletes possessing something that helps them succeed – their personalities'. However, the text does not say that they are born with high sensation-seeking

personalities. They could acquire or develop them over time.

3   YES The text says, 'To some extent we all crave complex and novel sensations … novelty tugs at us.'

6

4   YES The text says that 'high sensation-seeking individuals experience less stress and are fearless and calm in the face of danger'. There is also mention of the fact that people with high sensation-seeking personalities produce less cortisol, the stress hormone.

5   NO The text says the opposite of the statement – they produce 'higher levels of pleasure chemicals like dopamine' and 'have increased sensitivity to things that could be rewarding'. The text gives two examples of activities that involve a high level of risk and skill – the double cork 1080 and the triple axel.

6   NO Scientific research on sense sensation started in the 1950s and not the early twentieth century. The text says, 'In the 1950s, Canadian psychologists began studying sensory deprivation.'

7   YES The text says, 'During the first couple of hours of his study, all the research subjects simply sat there. But after that, things changed.'

8   YES The text says, 'People with low levels of disinhibition always look before they leap; they are cautious, unlike those with high disinhibition who will do the opposite.'

7   Test task

1   YES The text says, 'These discoveries have led to the field known as "neuroeconomics", <u>which studies the brain's secrets to success in an economic environment that demands innovation and being able to do things differently from competitors</u>.'

2   YES The text says, 'This definition implies that iconoclasts are different from other people, <u>but more precisely, it is their brains that are different in two ways: perception and fear response</u>.'

3   NO The text says, '<u>The brain takes shortcuts that work so well we are hardly ever aware of them</u>.'

4   YES The text says, 'Thus it [the brain] will <u>draw on both past experience and any other source of information, such as what other people say, to make sense of what it is seeing</u>.'

5   YES The text says, 'Successful iconoclasts have an extraordinary willingness to be exposed to what is fresh and different … they embrace novelty while most people avoid things that are different.'

6   NOT GIVEN The text says that '<u>most people avoid things that are different</u>' but it does not say that the reason for not trying new things is because of shyness.

7   NO The text says that people generally find it difficult to deal with 'fear of uncertainty' which means that iconoclasts do not have the ability to overcome fear easily.

8   NOT GIVEN The text makes reference to embarrassment in the phrase 'fear of public ridicule' but it does not say that other fears become irrelevant when people feel less concerned about it.

9   NO The text says the opposite. It says, 'This makes it too common to be considered a mental disorder' – a synonym for psychological illness.

Reading Worksheet 3

1

1   A (the text says that modern day air conditioning 'as we know it began in 1902')

2   A (There are over 7 billion people in the world but not all of them will have or need air conditioning. Therefore, the more likely answer is 4.5 billion.)

3   B (Air conditioners are basically just fridges but they make the space OUTSIDE them cool, while fridges keep the space INSIDE them cool.)

4   A (Air conditioners act as dehumidifiers – less humid air feels cooler.)

5   A

6   B

7   B

2

1 B

Section B tells us the date of the invention of the modern air conditioner, the name of the inventor and how he got his inspiration for the invention.

2 D

Section D tells us when the first domestic air conditioner was produced and it then goes on to talk about how popular they became all over America and why.

3 E

Section E tells us how important air conditioning is to different industries, museums, supermarkets, hospitals, schools, airports and offices – these are examples of how air conditioning has transformed modern living.

4 A

Section A tells us how early civilisations like the ancient Egyptians, ancient Babylonians and Romans tried to keep themselves cool.

5 C

Section C tells us that air conditioning was introduced into cinemas in the 1920s and we also learn that by 1930, more than 300 cinemas had installed them.

3

Section C focuses on what problems theatres had before the introduction of air conditioning.

4a

Singular noun: 3; 4; 6

Plural noun: 1; 2

Adjective: 5

4b

Gap 6 – we need a singular noun beginning with a vowel because the word preceding the gap is 'an'.

5a

'electricity' is incorrect for two reasons: the word doesn't fit grammatically – we can't say 'There were no electricity'.

'window' is incorrect grammatically. We need a plural form of the noun after 'were'.

'air conditioning' is incorrect for three reasons: one word must be used in the gap; a key word or words that are used across the text are not tested in the summary; the sentence before already makes reference to the fact there was no air conditioning in the theatres.

'windos' is incorrect because of its spelling.

5b

1 windows   2 Flares   3 summer   4 fan
5 unpleasant   6 attraction

6   Test task

The words you need come from the first three paragraphs of the text – the heading directs you to the second and third paragraphs as it focuses on Daguerre's experiments. The first paragraph is also needed because there is reference to Louis Pasteur. He is mentioned in the first sentence of the summary.

1   prepared mind.

We need an adjective and noun for the answer to fit the space and make sense in context. The text says, 'Louis Pasteur noted the additional requirement involved in serendipity when he said, 'chance favours only the prepared mind'. The words 'need to have' in the summary paraphrase 'additional requirement' given in the text.

2   iodine vapour

We need an adjective and noun for the answer to fit the space and make sense in context. The text says 'After adding a silver coating to the plate and exposing it to iodine vapour, he found that the photographic image was improved but still very weak.'

The words 'exposure to iodine vapour had the desired effect on a silver-coated photographic plate, but only to a very limited extent' in the summary paraphrase the underlined words above.

3   alcohol

We need an uncountable or a plural noun in the space to fit grammatically. The text says, 'in which laboratory chemicals such as alcohol and collodian were stored'. The word 'chemicals' is not suitable for the gap as collodian is given in the text as an example of a chemical. We couldn't therefore say 'chemicals and collodian' because of the word 'and'. Also, the word 'chemical' would not fit the space grammatically.

4   [spilt] mercury

We need an uncountable noun after the phrase 'amount of' to fit the space grammatically. The text says, 'Daguerre then noticed some spilt mercury on the cupboard shelf, and he concluded that this must have improved the photographic result.'

The summary paraphrases the underlined words: 'It was a small amount of spilt mercury that had produced the desired effect.'

Reading Worksheet 4

1

1   Canada (See Section A)
2   frozen dragon (See Section A)
3   76 million (See Section A)
4   giraffe (See Section E)
5   250 (See Section E)
6   10 (See Section E)
7   lizards/mammals (See Section E)
8   mammals/lizards (See Section E)
9   crocodiles (See Section E)

2a

ii

2b

Section A compares the climate of modern-day Alberta, Canada with the climate that Cryodrakon would have lived in. Nowadays the climate is much colder – the region is described as 'frozen desolate badlands'. But 'the area was as warm as the Mediterranean when Cryodrakon was alive'. Section A also mentions that crocodile fossils were also found in the region 'which always rule out very cold temperatures'.

3

1D

D talks about the special neck bones that makes Cyrodrakon different from all other azhdarchids. The way in which the bones were arranged were unique.

2C

C mentions that the dinosaur 'had suffered many battle wounds during its lifetime, with scratched bones and the tooth of a … meat-eating dinosaur imbedded in one of the fossils'.

3B

B talks about how scientists assumed that the fossils of Cryodrakon belonged to another pterosaur called Quetzalcoatlus.

4

Suggestions:

Cryodrakon's physical appearance, diet and way of moving – E

E gives a description of what Cryodrakon looked like, what it ate and how it moved.

Future direction of research into how Cryodrakon grew and moved – F

F talks about possible research to be carried out on Cryodrakon in future – including analysing its humerus in order to find out more about how it moved and analysis of thin sections of bones to find out how Cryodrakon grew from hatchling to adult.

5

Students' own answers

6

1 d   2 a   3 g   4 h   5 b   6 c   7 e   8 f

7

A   ii

'Although the fossils were unearthed in frozen, desolate badlands, the area was as warm as the Mediterranean when Cryodrakon boreas was alive.'

B   iv

'A couple of key advances prompted paleontologists to re-examine their views on Quetzalcoatlus.'

C   iii

'it had suffered many battle wounds during its lifetime'

D   vii

'He discovered that the formation of the pneumatophores, the holes through which the air sacs once entered the bone's interior, was unlike that of any other known azhdarchid.'

E   viii

In E we are told that Cryodrakon had enormous wings and that it 'used flight in order to escape danger or to seize its prey'. It also had a 'big head for guzzling things'. It was able to hunt 'baby dinosaurs, lizards and mammals'.

F   vi

In F we learn that scientists want to learn more about Cryodrakon and the section lists possible research areas that might be carried out in future. They want to find out more about how Cryodrakon moved and how it developed from hatchling to adult.

8 Test task

1   iii Ways in which people have responded to climate change over time

Paragraph A provides several examples of the way in which people responded to climate change over time. The text says, 'They developed strategies for surviving harsh drought cycles and decades of heavy rainfall or unaccustomed cold; they adopted agriculture and stock-raising, and founded the world's first pre-industrial civilisations in Egypt, Mesopotamia and the Americas.' Note that Paragraph D makes reference to 'how people in Europe adapted to' climatic shifts but gives no examples of ways in which they adapted.

2   ii The relevance of the Little Ice Age today

Paragraph B states that the Little Ice Age is very relevant to the world today. The text says, 'The climatic events of the Little Ice Age did more than help shape the modern world. They are the deeply important context for the current unprecedented global warming.'

3   v How past climatic conditions can be determined

Paragraph C gives a lot of information about how climatic conditions in the past can be determined. Information is provided by tree rings, ice cores and some written accounts. The text says, 'For the time before records began, we have only "proxy records" reconstructed largely from tree rings and ice cores, supplemented by a few incomplete written accounts. We now have hundreds of tree-ring records from throughout the northern hemisphere, and many from south of the equator too, amplified with a growing body of temperature data from ice cores drilled in Antartica, the Peruvian Andes, and other locations. We are close to a knowledge of annual summer and winter temperature variations over much of the northern hemisphere going back 600 years.'

4   iv A study covering a thousand years

Paragraph D talks about the time frame of the study. The text says, 'This book is a narrative history of climatic shifts during the past ten centuries, and details how people in Europe adapted to them.'

Writing Worksheet 1

1

1   Teachers' salaries (In 2000, they were 40%, 2010 they were 50% and 2020 they were 45%)
2   Insurance (I981 2%, 2010 3%, 2020 8%)
3   up (It went up slightly from 2% to 3% and then further to 8%)
4   big (It increased from 5% to 23%)
5   slight (8% on insurance and 9% on resources)
6   significant (20% to 9%)

2

1 e   2 d   3 a   4 c   5 b

3

1 Teachers' salaries   2 Insurance
3 Furniture and equipment   4 Other workers' salaries
5 Resources

4

1 decreased, declined, fell   2 significantly, dramatically
3 an upward trend

Get it right!

1 change 'slight' to 'slightly' and delete 'in'
2 change 'considerably' to 'considerable'

5

1 and 2 are both from introductions.

6

1 is much better because it uses synonyms for the words used in the question instead of using exactly the same words, which 2 does.

7

The pie charts show how much a UK school spent on different running costs in three separate years – 2000, 2010 and 2020.

8

1 most   2 least   3 broadly/largely the same
4 slightly less   5 much/far more, compared to/with

9

Suggested answer

The pie charts show how much a UK school spent on different running costs in three separate years – 2000, 2010 and 2020.

In all three years, the greatest expenditure was on staff salaries. But while other workers' salaries saw a dramatic fall from 28% to only 15% of spending in 2020, teachers' pay remained the biggest cost, reaching half of total spending in 2010 and ending at 45% in 2020.

Expenditure on resources such as books had increased to one fifth by 2010, before decreasing significantly to just 9% by the end of the period. In contrast, the cost of furniture and equipment saw an opposite trend. The cost decreased to only 5% of total expenditure in 2010 but rose dramatically in 2020 when it represented almost a quarter of the school budget. Similarly, the cost of insurance saw a rising trend, growing from only 2% to 8% by 2020.

Overall, teachers' salaries constituted the largest cost to the school, and while there was a dramatic increase in spending on equipment and insurance, there were corresponding drops in expenditure on things such as resources and other workers' salaries.

11 Test task

Suggested answer

The pie charts show how much energy is used in a typical Australian household and the amount of greenhouse gas emitted.

42% of energy is used for heating but this produces significantly fewer greenhouse gas emissions – only 15%. However, the reverse is true when it comes to the amount of energy used for refrigeration. This accounts for 7% of energy use but produces double the amount in terms of emissions. Lighting is similarly polluting in terms of emissions – producing 50% more greenhouse gas than it uses. Other appliances use 15% of energy but emit nearly double that percentage in greenhouse gas – at 28%.

There is very little difference in the quantity of emissions resulting from the use of cooling equipment. 2% of energy is used for this purpose and the resulting emissions are slightly higher at 3%. A similar small increase is evident in the emissions from water heating.

Overall, energy use on heating, lighting, refrigeration and other appliances results in nearly double the amount of greenhouse gas emissions, while energy use for cooling and water heating emits only slightly more greenhouse gas.

Writing Worksheet 2

1

True/T (There are four stages of life from hatching, becoming fry, becoming smolt and then reaching maturity as an adult salmon. There are three water environments – upper river, lower river and open sea as shown in the three separate boxes of the diagram. So, there are several physical stages.)

False/F (The salmon spends the early stages of its life in freshwater rivers as an egg, a fry and smolt. Its adult life is spent in open seas.]

False/F (The maximum length of an adult salmon is 76 centimetres.)

2

1 freshwater   2 fry   3 hatch   4 reeds   5 riverbed
6 saltwater   7 smolt   8 pebbles

3

4, 6, 7, 8

4   These are tall plants with a hollow stem that <u>are found</u> in or near water. (example]

6   This describes the water which <u>is found</u> in an open sea environment.

7   This term <u>is used</u> to describe a juvenile salmon.

8   These are smooth, round stones which <u>are found</u> in or near water.

4

The paragraph focuses on the later stage of the cycle when the salmon change from smolt into adults and then move into the open sea, before returning to their place of birth.

5a

When salmon fry reach a length of between twelve and fifteen centimetres, <u>they are then call</u> 'smolt', and at this <u>stages</u> of their lives <u>they are migrate</u> further downriver into the open sea. After five years <u>on</u> sea the salmon will have grown to adult size. They then <u>begins</u> swimming back to their place of birth <u>which</u> they will lay their eggs.

5b

When salmon fry reach a length of between twelve and fifteen centimetres, <u>they are then called</u> [passive] 'smolt', and at this stage [singular/plural noun] of their lives <u>they migrate</u> [active / present simple] further downriver into the open sea. After five years <u>at</u> [preposition] sea the salmon will have grown to adult size. They then <u>begins</u> [active / present simple] swimming back to their place of birth <u>where</u> [relative clause] they will lay their eggs.

6a

The overview is at the end of the answer. It begins with the phrase 'In summary'.

6b

Yes, the student follows all the advice given in the checklist in the Test tip.

7

Suggested answer

Salmon begin life as eggs on a riverbed of pebbles which are hidden among reeds in a slow-moving upper river. After a period of five to six months, the eggs hatch into 'fry'. For the next four years approximately, these baby salmon will be found in the lower faster-flowing waters of their river. During this time they measure between three and eight centimetres in length.

By the time salmon reach 12 to 15 centimetres, they are termed 'smolt', and at this time they migrate further downriver into the open sea. After five years at sea, the salmon will have grown to adult size, which is between 70 and 76 centimetres. They then begin swimming back to their place of birth where they will lay their eggs.

In summary, the diagrams show how the salmon passes through four distinct physical stages. This involves hatching out of an egg, growing into fry and then smolt before becoming an adult salmon. In the first three stages of its life, the fish inhabits a freshwater environment in slow-moving and then fast-moving rivers while the final stage of its life cycle is spent in saltwater.

8 Test task

Suggested answer

The first stage in the production of cement involves placing limestone and clay into a crusher so that the hard stones become powder. The material is then deposited into a mixer and passed through a special rotating heater. After heating to the required temperature, the mixture is placed through a grinder which turns it into cement. The cement is then packed into bags.

In order to produce concrete, a number of different materials are poured into a concrete mixer. Half of the material used to make concrete is gravel, or small stones. This is combined with sand and cement in different quantities. Water is added and the materials are mixed together.

In summary, the diagrams show how the cement and concrete are produced. The production of cement involves several steps; namely crushing, mixing, heating and griding before being placed in bags. However, there are fewer materials involved – only limestone and clay. Concrete production requires the use of more materials but consists of fewer stages. The materials are simply mixed together in different quantities and no heating is involved.

Writing Worksheet 3

1a
1 Picture B   2 Picture C   3 Picture A

1b
a exhibits   b interactive   c souvenir   d collection
e jewellery   f on display   g accessible   h life-size
i sculpture   j preserving

2b
B

3
Students' own notes

4b
View 1: 1, 3, 5   View 2: 2, 4

5
4:   Some people think that

6
Students' own notes

7
1 E   2 D   3 B   4 C   5 A

8b
1   The writer supports the first view – the view that admission charges are fair and reasonable.

2   The writer mentions Statement 1 in Exercise 4a about museums being expensive to run and also Statement 5 about people having to pay for other leisure activities.

3   Yes, in Paragraph 2. The writer makes reference to Statement 4 in Exercise 4a that admission charges could deter poorer people from going to museums.

4   Yes, the writer mentions that museums are free of charge on Mondays in their home city.

8c
1 D   2 B   3 A   4 C

9
Students' own paragraphs

10b
A

11
Students' own paragraphs

12 Test task

Suggested answer

Many schools organise trips and excursions to a variety of cultural institutions, including art galleries, natural history and science museums, as well as theatres, wildlife parks and historical sites. Some people take the view that these kinds of visits can enhance learning, while others think that a student's time is best spent within a classroom setting. I firmly believe that these visits should be compulsory.

Some people argue that trips and excursions may distract students from their coursework and their progress towards examinations. However, many museums provide events that are relevant to subjects taught in school. For example, in my city, there is an annual Science Festival which includes interactive workshops on many of the topics covered in subjects like Physics.

However, there is no doubt that students can learn a great deal by learning outside the confines of the classroom. A visit to a Science Festival event can enable students to interact with a variety of different exhibits – such as a wave machine. These can help bring the subject to life and enable students to 'learn by doing'. Furthermore, they can contribute to the development of students into mature adults with the critical thinking and problem-solving skills they will need in their future lives. Finally, it is impossible to argue against the fact that learning is about more than examination success. Surely schools have a responsibility to promote a love of learning for its own sake. For example, a visit to a concert might encourage a lifelong passion for classical music.

All in all, I strongly believe that these kinds of trips

should form an integral part of high school programmes. Schools have a responsibility to ensure that students have exposure to the world around them and what better way to do this than to step outside the classroom.

Writing Worksheet 4

1

Students' own answers

2b

A review

3a

C is the most positive as it doesn't mention any negative aspects. A and B mention both advantages and disadvantages.

4

1 B   2 A   3 A, C   4 B   5 B   6 C   7 A, C

5

1 A   2 B   3 A   4 A

6

drawback   on the plus side

7a

Students' own answers

7b

1 positive   2 yes   3 false

7c

a   In other words
b   For instance [For example]
c   Another good point [thing] / One advantage [benefit]
d   One final benefit [advantage] [positive aspect] is
e   For instance [For example]
f   One drawback [issue] [downside] is
g   One other issue [drawback] [downside] is
h   For instance [For example]

8

Conclusion A follows both tips. It is better because the student includes their own opinion. (Also B throws in an additional point about eye strain at the end which should really have been mentioned in the main body, and just summarised here, e.g. *However, it is important to remember that there are drawbacks too, such as eye strain and the battery running out.*)

9

Suggested answer

These days, an increasing number of people are using e-readers instead of printed books. There are a number of reasons why these electronic devices are becoming more popular.

One of the best things about e-readers is that they are much more portable compared to printed books. To put it another way, they can be slipped in a bag and carried about very easily. Furthermore, unlike printed books, many e-readers are waterproof so you do not have to worry if you accidentally drop your device in the sea. One other positive aspect is that you can download e-books very cheaply and sometimes even a whole chapter of a book for free. For instance, I sometimes read a sample of an e-book before buying it.

However, there are some disadvantages to e-readers. Some people may find it uncomfortable to read a book on a screen for long periods. However, there are devices available which enable you to adjust the size of the words and the brightness of the screen. Another drawback is that you do not have the pleasure of holding a physical book in your hand. However, there are some e-readers that provide a flipping animation. For example, I have an app on my device that enables me to experience the sound and sight of the page turning in front of me on the screen.

On balance, I believe that the benefits of e-readers outweigh the drawbacks. We live in an ever-changing world and the ability to read wherever and whenever we want offers a great deal of convenience. I am convinced that they are a positive development – not only do they make our lives easier, but they are better for the environment too – they help to conserve valuable paper resources and they take up less space!

10   Test task

Suggested answer

These days, an increasing number of people are listening to audio books instead of reading printed books. There are a number of reasons for this trend.

One of the best things about audio books is that they are extremely convenient. For example, you can listen to your favourite novel when you are standing on a crowded bus or when you are driving on the motorway. Another advantage is that there is such a wide variety of audio books available to download nowadays and they are often considerably cheaper than printed books. One final positive aspect about audio books is that you can simply close your eyes and enjoy a story from beginning to end – you will not suffer from the effects of eye strain that can happen when reading a paperback for long periods.

However, there are some disadvantages to audio books. Some people may lose concentration while listening and find it difficult to return to the correct part of the story. Another drawback is that you do not have the pleasure of handling a physical book in your hand. One final downside is that you may actually not like the voice of the reader in the audio book. However, there are many audio books available which feature a range of voices and sound effects which help to immerse the listener fully in the story.

On balance, I believe that the benefits of audio books outweigh the drawbacks. Talking books give people more choice in how they enjoy a book. Whether they choose to listen or read does not really matter. The experience is the most important thing.

Writing Worksheet 5

1

You are being asked to say whether you agree or disagree with governments imposing a higher tax on short domestic flights.

2

1 domestic tourism   2 green energy
3 sustainable travel   4 air pollution   5 eco-friendly
6 diesel fuel   7 global warming
8 offsetting your emissions   9 large carbon footprint

3

Good for the environment: domestic tourism, eco-friendly, green energy, offsetting your emissions, sustainable travel

Bad for environment: air pollution, diesel fuel, global warming, large carbon footprint

4b

C (I firmly believe that tackling the problem of global warming needs far more than a simple tax to make people reconsider how they travel.)

5

1 A / agree   2 D / disagree   3 A / agree
4 A / agree   5 D/ disagree

6

1 C   2 E   3 A   4 D   5 B

7

1 despite   2 although, despite   3 but
4 Nevertheless, However

Get it right!

1 Although fewer flights would mean more trains, this could place pressure on the rail network.
2 Travelling by rail or bus may take longer than flying, but you get to see more of the country than you would by sitting on a plane.

8

Students' own answers

9a

Main idea: People living in remote areas don't have a choice of travel.

9b

despite   Although   but   Nevertheless

10

Students' own answers

11

Governments could encourage airlines to design planes that use greener fuels.

Invest more in bus and rail services

Educate people about sustainable travel

12

Suggested answer

There is no doubt that an increasing number of people are choosing to take domestic flights these days and this is having a serious impact on the environment. This is because these individual short trips can have a remarkably large carbon footprint. However, despite the high CO2 emissions emitted, I strongly believe that tackling the problem of climate change is likely to need more than a simple tax.

Although there can be no doubt that short flights are responsible for a lot of carbon emissions, imposing a tax is unlikely to discourage people from flying short distances – particularly those who live in remote areas and have no other option but to fly. Furthermore, it is sometimes the case that it is cheaper for travellers to fly than to take the train or the car.

Nevertheless, there are various other measures that could help to reduce greenhouse gas emissions. Firstly, governments could persuade airlines to design planes which have more efficient engines and use cleaner fuels. Furthermore, there needs to be more investment in improving bus and rail services and ensuring that these run efficiently. Finally, I think that there is a need for more education about the effects of global warming and how cutting back on air travel could have a positive impact. Some people simply do not realise just how polluting short flights are.

In conclusion, I think that imposing a tax on domestic flights would have a limited impact on addressing the serious issue of climate change. It is far more useful to educate the public about the importance of sustainable travel and for governments to construct and run efficient rail and bus systems.

13 Test task

Suggested answer

There is no doubt that traffic and pollution from vehicles have become huge problems, both in cities and on motorways everywhere. Solving these problems is likely to need more than a simple rise in the price of petrol.

Although private car use is one of the main causes of the increase in traffic and pollution, higher fuel costs are unlikely to limit the number of drivers for long. Increasing the price of fuel may also have an impact on the cost of public transport – bus companies would likely expect customers to pay higher fares to help fund the extra fuel costs. This would be extremely unpopular with everyone who needs to travel on the roads. But there are various other measures that could be implemented that would have a huge effect on these problems.

In my opinion, to tackle the problem of pollution, cleaner fuels need to be developed. The technology is already available to produce electric cars that would be both quieter and cleaner to use. Persuading manufacturers and travellers to adopt this new technology would be a more effective strategy for improving air quality, especially in cities.

However, traffic congestion will not be solved by changing the type of private vehicle people can use. To do this, we need to improve the choice of public transport services available to travellers. For example, if more bus stations and underground train systems were built and effectively maintained in our major cities, then traffic on the roads would be dramatically reduced.

In conclusion, I think that long-term traffic and pollution reductions would depend on promoting the use of cleaner technology and on government using public money to construct and run efficient public transport systems.

Speaking Worksheet 1

1

1 alike   2 like   3 like doing   4 look like / like

NARRATOR:	Track 31 Speaking Worksheet 1
EXAMINER:	Are you and your friends alike?
	What are your family like?
	What do you and your friends like doing together?
	Who, in your family, do you look like most?

2

1 D   2 B   3 A   4 C

NARRATOR:	Track 32 Speaking Worksheet 1
NARRATOR:	1
EXAMINER:	Are you and your friends alike?
STUDENT:	I'm like my best friend Martha. We're both quite impatient and when it comes to sports, we're very competitive as we hate losing.

NARRATOR:	2
EXAMINER:	What are your family like?
STUDENT:	Well, mum's tall and elegant and, um, quite strict – especially about things like keeping my room tidy, or when I want to stay out late with my mates.
NARRATOR:	3
EXAMINER:	What do you and your friends like doing together?
STUDENT:	A It depends on the weather really. If it's nice, we love chilling out in the park. It helps us relax after a hard day at college.
NARRATOR:	4
EXAMINER:	Who, in your family, do you look like most?
STUDENT:	That'll be my dad. Our features are very similar; for example, we've got the same chin and nose.

3

1   X In English, it is generally considered rude to say 'What?' if you do not hear what someone has said to you.

2   OK In English, 'Pardon?' means that you did not hear what someone has said to you.

3   OK In English, 'Sorry' has several meanings. One meaning is that you did not hear what someone has said to you.

4   X It is not natural to say 'Repeat?' if you do not hear what someone has said to you. If you want to use 'repeat', you should use it in a phrase, for example, 'Could you repeat that please?'

4

2   Could you repeat the question?

3   Would you mind saying that again please?

NARRATOR:	Track 33 Speaking Worksheet 1
STUDENT:	I didn't quite catch that. Could you say it again please?
	Sorry, I missed that. Could you repeat the question?
	I couldn't quite hear you. Would you mind saying that again please?

5

1 B   2 A   3 D   4 C

NARRATOR: **Track 34**
Speaking Worksheet 1

NARRATOR: A

EXAMINER: What do you like about your home town or city?

STUDENT: Well, there's a lot to do which is great. My best friend and I often go to the cinema. Last week we saw a 3D film. It was amazing. The special effects were super cool and the acting superb. My favourite genre of film is horror. I just love it, you know, when a film makes me jump out of my seat in fear.

NARRATOR: B

EXAMINER: Do you think your hometown has changed much in recent years?

STUDENT: Not really, no.

EXAMINER: Why not?

STUDENT: I dunno.

NARRATOR: C

EXAMINER: Is your hometown a popular place for tourists to visit?

STUDENT: Yes, it's a popular holiday destination. Mainly due to our amazing sandy beach and then there are great cultural attractions, like the castle ruins and the museum.

NARRATOR: D

EXAMINER: Do you prefer the summer or winter in your hometown?

STUDENT: That's an interesting question. I was talking to my friend about this last week. While some would argue that summer is the best time of year, in my opinion, I prefer winter.

6

Words and phrases to give examples	Words and phrases to give reasons
for instance	as
like	due to
including	since
such as	this happens because

7

1 B   2 E   3 C   4 G   5 A   6 D   7 F

8 Test task

Example notes:

1 like football / as I get to keep fit / spend time with mates

2 football as footballing nation / cycling for instance / due to success in the Tour de France

Laya didn't say what she would personally like to try, but instead talks about what's popular in her country.

3 Occasionally, if it was an important international match, like the World Cup / always preferred to go outside

4 Laya uses the phrase, 'I didn't quite catch that' to let the examiner know she didn't hear the question clearly.

football at primary school / … including tennis and basketball at senior school / almost all senior schools have a basketball team, for example

NARRATOR: **Track 35**
Speaking Worksheet 1

EXAMINER: Let's talk about sports. Do you enjoy playing sports?

LAYA: Yes, I do. I particularly like taking part in team sports, like football, as I get to keep fit and also spend time with my mates.

EXAMINER: Is there any sport you would you like to try in the future?

LAYA: Well, I'd have to say football is the most popular sport as we're a footballing nation, although more recently other sports, um, cycling for instance, have become really popular. Cycling is due to our success in the Tour de France, I expect.

EXAMINER: Do you often watch sport on TV?

LAYA: No, I didn't, not really. I mean, occasionally, if it was an important international football match, like the World Cup um since I love football … but to be honest, I've always preferred to go outside and play football rather than watching it indoors.

EXAMINER: What sports do children normally do at school in your country?

LAYA: Sorry, I didn't quite catch that. Did you say 'at school'?

EXAMINER: Yes, that's right.

LAYA: Hm well, when I was at school, there was football of course and children of all ages get taught that – even in primary school. Then, at senior school, kids can play other sports including tennis and basketball. I think almost all senior schools have a basketball team, for example.

EXAMINER: Thank you.

9

Students' own answers

Speaking Worksheet 2

1

See underlining in Track 36.
1 A   2 B   3 B   4 A   5 B

NARRATOR: **Track 36**
Speaking Worksheet 2

CHANGYING: Hey Abbas. How's it going?

ABBAS: Hello Changying. I'm good. Just trying to revise for my IELTS Speaking test next week.

CHANGYING: I'm struggling with my revision.

ABBAS: Why?

CHANGYING: Well, it's Part Two that's keeping me awake at night.

ABBAS: Ah you're worried because you're not sure what to say for two minutes?

CHANGYING: Well, there is that though it's more about speaking alone, <u>specifically without any questions from the examiner</u>.

ABBAS: I know what you mean; however, there's a task card isn't there, plus what's really useful is you get a minute to prepare what you want to talk about.

CHANGYING: I guess.

ABBAS: What revision strategies are you using?

CHANGYING: Right well, <u>I think it's good to memorise answers – that way you can use the same vocabulary and phrases no matter what</u>.

ABBAS: <u>I'm not sure that's an effective use of revision time</u>. It's unlikely you'll get the same topic in the real test and you'll just sound unnatural. I think knowing how to correctly talk about the past, present and future, as well as being fluent, is the best option.

CHANGYING: Ah you might be right.

ABBAS: What about pronunciation?

CHANGYING: Hmm I guess I could improve that by <u>recording and listening to myself which I reckon is better than listening to local people</u>.

ABBAS: I also think it is a good idea to time yourself answering a Part Two question.

CHANGYING: Why's that?

ABBAS: Well, <u>so you get to know what speaking for one to two minutes feels like</u>. When you're answering the question in the test, you'll probably be too nervous to think about that.

CHANGYING: I agree. Is it OK to tell a lie – you know make something up?

ABBAS: Well, you won't lose marks, but if you ask me, the best answers are about real personal experiences.

CHANGYING: You're right. That way I might feel a bit more confident about <u>expanding on my ideas, you know, by giving examples for instance</u>.

ABBAS: Don't forget if you talk about something that's happened, or will happen; then you'll sound more natural too.

2

See underlining in Track 37.
1 wanted me to talk about   2 with that in mind
3 the sort of people who typically   4 Regarding its
5 about the reason

NARRATOR: **Track 37**
Speaking Worksheet 2

CHANGYING: <u>You wanted me to talk about a local shop I go to every so often. So, with that in mind, I'm going to talk about a shop called New From Old</u> which sells furniture like coffee tables, chairs and lamp shades. I think the <u>sort of people who typically go there are</u> people **like my Aunt Miriam, for example**. She's a designer. Actually, she designs and makes cushions from old sheets and jumpers which she sells in New From Old. Anyway, **it's people like her who tend to go**

---

there because the stuff they sell is so unique and I think designers and, you know, creative people like that. Regarding its location, it's not far from where I live in the old part of the city.

When I say not far, **I mean** I can walk there from home in around twenty minutes.

There are a lot of, well, arty shops in the same street. You know, erm, such as shops that sell artisan bread, hand-made jewellery ... So, it's located in a good spot, I think. What about the reason why I like shopping in New From Old? Well, **as I said**, Aunt Miriam's cushions are sold there, **but it's more than that**. New From Old is all about recycling and reusing, for example, they take things that people are going to throw away, like an old table and they give it new life. You know, **they repair it**, paint it vibrant colours and then sell it to someone who does want it. I bought a lamp from them last week and it was made from old tyres which were painted white. I mean amazing, right?

So that's why I go there really – it takes things that no one wants anymore and turns them into something special and as I don't agree with waste – well, I think it's a super idea for a shop.

3

See **bold** text in Track 37.

1 C   2 A   3 H   4 G   5 B   6 F   7 E

D is not needed.

4

When writing notes, do not try and write down everything you want to say. Instead think about a few detailed phrases and ideas that you can expand on when you are speaking. Whatever note-taking style you use, your notes should be clear enough to follow. Remember, IELTS Part 2 is not a test of knowledge but a test of how you communicate about a topic, so use the one minute you have before you start speaking to write notes effectively.

5

Example notes:

What: Sports car / Porsche 918 718 Boxster to be precise

How long: early teens / around 10 years ago

Where: Not (entirely) sure / out walking with dad / local park / used to be a football coach

Why: You might think looks: low & sleek / however: deep sound / performance: premium car / I'll be a proud owner

---

NARRATOR: 🔊 Track 38
Speaking Worksheet 2

ABBAS: Right, well the thing I really would like to have that I don't already is a sports car. A Porsche 718 Boxster, to be precise. I reckon the first time I saw one, I was in my early teens, about thirteen or fourteen years old, so around ten years ago now. As for where? Well, to be honest, I'm not entirely sure – I was out walking with my dad, so I think it was near the local park. Yeah, that's right, we were on our way back from playing football – my dad used to be the team coach – and it just went past us.

You might think it's the way it looks, you know, low, two-seater, sleek; however, actually, it's the sound it makes. That sort of deep rumble. I just love it. Then of course, it's the performance. I've read about it since, and the Boxster is a premium car. At least that's what I think and that's the reason why one day, once I've saved and saved, I'll be the proud owner of one.

---

6 Test task

Students' own answers

Speaking Worksheet 3

1

A   Which skills should children learn at school? / At school, which skills should children learn? / Children should learn which skills at school?

B   Are there any skills which they should learn at home?

C   Which skills and abilities will be important in the future? / Which abilities and skills will be important in the future? / In the future which skills and abilities will be important? / In the future which abilities and skills will be important?

2

See underlining in Track 39.

Techniques for developing ideas:	✓ / ✗	Explanation
1 giving your own point of view or opinion	✓	'seems to me' and 'Personally': the speaker is providing their own opinion.
2 giving others' points of view or ideas	✓	'some might say': the speaker is providing hypothetical opinions of unnamed people.
3 suggesting a solution to a problem	✓	'one way of dealing with this': the speaker has provided a problem and has suggested one solution is to 'teach life skills'.
4 explaining why something happens	✓	'Because of this' and 'instance': the speaker provides two explanations.
5 offering a contrasting idea	✗	The speaker doesn't provide any contrasting ideas.
6 making future predictions	✓	'likely to need': the speaker is predicting that we're 'likely to need' technology skills to deal with a changing world.
7 explaining advantages and/or disadvantages of something	✓	'Technology offers us, and the planet, huge potential benefits': the Speaker says that technology is a 'huge' 'benefit', meaning an advantage. However, the word 'potential' can imply that there could be disadvantages (these are not named or further explained).
8 giving examples to support ideas	✓	'as an example': the Speaker provides an example of socialising to support the argument.
9 giving factual information	✗	The Speaker provides no quoted, factual information. Everything mentioned is based on personal opinion and hypothetical ideas.

NARRATOR: 🔊 **Track 39**
Speaking Worksheet 3

EXAMINER: We've been talking about skills and abilities, and I'd like to ask you a few more questions. So, first of all, which skills do you think children should learn at school?

BERDINE: Well, it <u>seems to me</u> that children don't behave as well as they used to, and one way <u>of dealing with</u> this is to teach life skills. Let's take socialising <u>as an example</u>. Children these days spend too much time in front of computers. <u>Because of this,</u> they don't know how to properly form relationships face to face – socialise with their peers, communicate – things like that. So, I think schools ought to pick it up.

EXAMINER: Right, thank you. So, are there any skills which children should learn at home?

BERDINE: Hm, well <u>some might say</u> that life skills, or specifically the social skills I mentioned before, ought to be taught at home, but that's not always possible for one reason or another. Um for <u>instance</u>, they may have no siblings or even friends nearby to play with. <u>Personally,</u> I think children should learn from their parents how to love and respect themselves and others. That's really important, you know, for a child's future.

EXAMINER: I see, and which skills and abilities will be important in the future?

BERDINE: Hm, let me think. Right well, technology is advancing all the time, isn't it? The world is really changing. So, I think we're <u>likely to need</u> skills related to that. So, IT programming and computer design and creativity and well, we need to be able to solve complex problems, things like that, to tackle issues like global warming. <u>Technology offers us, and the planet, huge potential benefits</u>, so developing any skills and abilities related to that will be the most important.

3

See underlining in Track 39.

1 seems to me   2 of dealing with   3 as an example.

4 Because of this 5 some might say 6 instance
7 Personally 8 likely to need 9 huge potential benefits

4

1 giving others' points of view or ideas
2 discussing advantages and/or disadvantages of something
3 giving examples to support ideas
4 suggesting a solution to a problem
5 giving your own point of view or opinion
6 making future predictions
7 offering a contrasting idea
8 giving factual information
9 explaining why something happens

5

Disagree	Neither disagree nor agree	Agree
I'm not so sure about that.	That depends on the situation.	My thoughts exactly.
That's not the way I see it.	I think we need to consider both sides.	There's no doubt about it.

6

1 Advik neither agrees nor disagrees with the opinion.
2 Advik uses the phrase, 'I'm in two minds' to express his view.
3 In agreement: Advik develops his ideas by using the example of a footballer's salary and a doctor's salary and says it would be 'fairer' if they were paid the same: 'doctors save lives … if someone needs major heart surgery'.

   In disagreement: Advik uses a firefighter and aircraft pilot as examples of jobs which people might not want to do if all salaries were equal.

NARRATOR: 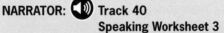 Track 40
            Speaking Worksheet 3

EXAMINER: Some people say it would be better for society if everyone got the same salary. What do you think about that?

ADVIK: Well, to be honest, I'm in two minds about that really. I can see if we were to all get paid the same, then things might feel fairer; take a footballer's salary compared to a doctor's, for example. I mean, footballers get paid vast amounts of money to kick a ball whereas doctors get paid a lot less to save lives … You know, if someone needs major heart surgery,

---

something like that. On the other hand, if all salaries were equal, then people might not want to do challenging or high-risk jobs like becoming a firefighter or aircraft pilot.

---

7 Test task

Students' own answers

Get it right!

RAJ:

Well, I don't believe that having a lot of possessions will necessarily equal success in the future. For me, being successful will be about having a happy and healthy family rather than the number of items I own.

This is not the best candidate response. Although the candidate talks about whether owning possessions in the future will be a sign of success and gives a supporting example, their answer is personal and does not discuss the views of other people generally.

MARIA:

Not really, no. I think the focus on having good mental health will continue and for many, success will be more about living a stress-free life, for example, less work and more family time, than buying flash cars.

This is the best candidate response. The candidate discusses a possible view of other people and speaks generally, 'the focus on having good mental health will … for many (for many people)'. A supporting example is given.

HANU:

Absolutely. My dad really wants to own a premium car, like a Lamborghini, in the future. He thinks it will show other people how successful he is. I'd like lots of expensive possessions in the future too.

This is not the best answer. Although the candidate talks about the future and the connection between owning possessions and success, the candidate uses a personal example, (dad), and does not discuss the views of other people generally.

Think about it

Listening Worksheet 1

1 in the order you hear them
2 don't choose
3 Word matching
4 the same idea / a different way
5 will
6 Only one
7 once
8 speaker

Listening Worksheet 2

1 TRUE
2 TRUE
3 FALSE
4 FALSE (always follow not sometimes)
5 TRUE
6 FALSE Keep listening and continue to the next question.
7 FALSE There will always be options you do not need.
8 TRUE

Listening Worksheet 3

1 h
2 d
3 b
4 g
5 c
6 a
7 e
8 f

Listening Worksheet 4

1 monologue
2 directions
3 location
4 tourist
5 question
6 letters
7 compass
8 orientate

Listening Worksheet 5

1 TRUE
2 FALSE Your answer will be marked wrong.
3 FALSE Your answer will be marked wrong.
4 TRUE
5 FALSE They may appear in any part of the test.
6 FALSE You will be asked to complete a gap.
7 TRUE
8 TRUE

Listening Worksheet 6

1 might hear
2 correct answer
3 unanswered
4 Guess
5 specific
6 the exact
7 Use
8 follow

Reading Worksheet 1

1 reading
2 idea
3 phrase
4 section
5 options
6 underline
7 words
8 text

Reading Worksheet 2

1 FALSE See Question 2.
2 TRUE
3 FALSE They will not be stated directly.
4 FALSE For some questions you may need to read the whole text.
5 FALSE NO statements contradict the claims of the writer.
6 TRUE
7 FALSE The exact number of YES, NO and NOT GIVEN answers will vary.
8 TRUE

Reading Worksheet 3

1 may
2 the exact
3 must not
4 have to
5 may not
6 type of word
7 before
8 one section

Reading Worksheet 4

1 b
2 h
3 d
4 g
5 f
6 e
7 c
8 a

Writing Worksheet 1

1 will
2 20
3 a formal
4 must not
5 150
6 to make
7 the main features
8 too few

Writing Worksheet 2

1 describe
2 overview
3 paragraph
4 information
5 stages
6 sentences
7 well-organised
8 academic

Writing Worksheet 3

1 FALSE You must answer both questions.
2 TRUE
3 FALSE Use a formal and academic style.
4 FALSE Write a minimum of 250 words.
5 TRUE
6 TRUE
7 FALSE It should include an introduction and a conclusion.
8 TRUE

Writing Worksheet 4

1 b
2 h
3 a
4 c
5 d
6 f
7 e
8 g

Writing Worksheet 5

1 two
2 must
3 linking words
4 despite
5 will
6 important
7 task response
8 paragraphs

Speaking Worksheet 1

1 familiar
2 dislikes
3 naturally
4 reasons
5 repeat
6 penalised
7 correct
8 five

Speaking Worksheet 2

1 g
2 a
3 e
4 h
5 c
6 f
7 b
8 d

Speaking Worksheet 3

1 FALSE You can agree, disagree or partially agree with an opinion given in the question.
2 TRUE
3 FALSE It lasts four to five minutes.
4 FALSE It is important to develop ideas with reasons, examples and solutions.
5 TRUE
6 FALSE It is fine to give factual information.
7 TRUE
8 TRUE

ACKNOWLEDGEMENTS

The authors and publishers acknowledge the following sources of copyright material and are grateful for the permissions granted. While every effort has been made, it has not always been possible to identify the sources of all the material used, or to trace all copyright holders. If any omissions are brought to our notice, we will be happy to include the appropriate acknowledgements on reprinting and in the next update to the digital edition, as applicable.

Key: RWK = Reading Worksheet, LWK = Listening Worksheet, WWK = Writing Worksheet, SWK = Speaking Worksheet.

Text

RWK1: Immediate Media for the text adapted from 'BBC Wildlife, Seahorses in the Bahamas' by Helena Scales. Copyright © 2019 Immediate Media. Reproduced with permission; New Scientist Ltd for the text adapted from 'The ancestor within all creatures' by Michael Le Page, 10.1.2007. Copyright © 2007 New Scientist Ltd. All rights reserved. Distributed by Tribune Content Agency; **RWK2:** Kenneth Carter for the text adapted from 'How a thrill-seeking personality helps Olympic athletes' by Kenneth Carter, The Conversation, 10.2.2018. Copyright © Kenneth Carter. Reproduced with kind permission; **RWK3:** Harvard Business Publishing for the text adapted from 'Iconoclast: A Neuroscientist Reveals How to Think Differently' by Gregory Berns, 2.9.2008. Copyright © Harvard Business Publishing. Produced with permission; John Wiley & Son for the text adapted from 'Serendipity: accidental discoveries in science' by Royston M Roberts, Copyright © 1989. Republished with permission of John Wiley & Son. Permission conveyed through Copyright Clearance Center, Inc.; **RWK4:** Hachette Books Group for the text adapted from 'The little ice age: how climate made history 1300–1850' by Brian M Fagan, Copyright © 2001. Republished with permission of Hachette Books Group. Permission conveyed through Copyright Clearance Center, Inc.

Photography

The following images have been sourced from Getty Images.

RWK1: GOLFX/iStock/Getty Images Plus; **RWK2:** Score/Aflo; Luxy Images; sutiporn somnam/Moment; PeopleImages/iStock/Getty Images Plus; **LWK1:** Stephen Frink/The Image Bank; **LWK2:** fstop123/E+; franckreporter/E+; Poike/iStock/Getty Images Plus; **LWK3:** guruXOOX/iStock Getty Images Plus; **LWK4:** Artur Debat/Moment; John Lund/Photodisc; Francesco Bergamaschi/Moment; **LWK5:** Image Source; EThamPhoto/The Image Bank; Poshey Aherne/500px; **SWK1:** Jack Hollingsworth; **SWK2:** 10'000 Hours/DigitalVision; **WWK3:** Stanislav_Moroz/iStock/Getty Images Plus; Stockbyte; Romilly Lockyer/The Image Bank; **WWK4:** Atstock Productions/iStock/Getty Images Plus; Indeed; **WWK5:** guvendemir/iStock/Getty Images Plus.

Audio

Audio production by Sounds Like Mike.

Typesetting

Typeset by Blooberry Design.

The publishers would also like to thank the following for their contributions to this project: Trish Chapman; Judith Wilson and Carole Allsop.